Holy Spirit, My Love!

Holy Spirit, My Love!

The Biography of the Holy Spirit

SUDONG KIM

Resource *Publications*

An imprint of *Wipf and Stock Publishers*
199 West 8th Avenue • Eugene OR 97401

HOLY SPIRIT, MY LOVE!
The Biography of the Holy Spirit

Copyright © 2007 Sudong Kim. All rights reserved. Except for brief quotations in critical publications or reviews, no part of this book may be reproduced in any manner without prior written permission from the publisher. Write: Permissions, Wipf and Stock, 199 W. 8th Ave., Eugene, OR 97401.

Translated by Sudong Kim from the Korean edition, Na eui Sa Rang, SUNG RYUNG NIM, published by Qumran Publishing Co. Ltd., Copyright © 2005.

Unless otherwise indicated, Scripture quotations are from the Holy Bible, New International Version Copyright © 1973, 1978, 1984 by the International Bible Society.

ISBN 13: 978-1-55635-388-8

Manufactured in the U.S.A.

Dedicated to the Holy Spirit, my love!

Contents

Foreword   ix

1: Prologue   1
2: Good Morning, Holy Spirit!   5
3: Who Are You, Holy Spirit?   10
4: The Holy Spirit and the Trinity   15
5: Other Titles of the Holy Spirit   28
6: The Symbols of the Holy Spirit   34
7: The Holy Spirit and Creation   36
8: The Holy Spirit and Salvation   39
9: The Holy Spirit and Sealing   50
10: The Holy Spirit and Regeneration   52
11: The Holy Spirit and Baptism   61
12: The Holy Spirit and the Church   77
13: The Double Works of the Holy Spirit   84
14: The Fruit of the Holy Spirit   95
15: The Spiritual Gifts of the Holy Spirit   97
16: The Fullness of the Holy Spirit   101
17: All the Works of the Holy Spirit   104
18: The Name of the Holy Spirit   108
19: The Holy Spirit and Christ   124
20: The Holy Spirit and the Word   128
21: Holy Spirit, My Love!   137

Epilogue   145
Bibliography   151

Foreword

Korean churches today are rather confused because of over-flooded pneumatologies. Therefore, there is an urgent need for Korean ministers and pastors to understand correctly regarding God, the Holy Spirit. I am very glad to note that Pastor Sudong Kim draws from his graduate thesis to write this book, *Holy Spirit, My Love!* and that it is edited to be easily understood by everyone.

The book is constructed in narrative form explaining concepts using simple words and avoiding theological or academic terminology. Pastor Sudong Kim emphasizes that we can, and should, call upon the Holy Spirit just like we call upon God the Father and Jesus.

Above all things, this book deeply illustrates—from the conservative and reformed point of view—how God the Holy Spirit is revealed in the Bible. For example, he regards "Baptism with the Holy Spirit" and "Sealing with the Holy Spirit" as having the same meaning as "Born again with the Holy Spirit."

Pastor Sudong Kim has done an excellent job of arranging his ideas regarding the basic substance of the Holy Spirit, as well as the relationship between the Holy Spirit and creation, salvation, regeneration, baptism, church, gifts, fruit, fullness, etc.

John Eui Whan Kim, PhD
President, Calvin University and Seminary

1

Prologue

Since January 2000, I have been presenting bi-annual pneumatology seminars to pastors and ministers in Burkina Faso, West Africa. Early on, before starting each lecture, I would ask: "My dear co-workers, do you believe in God?"

A few hundred pastors would shout, "Amen!" in loud voices.

I then asked: "Is there anybody who has seen God?" Silence hung in the air as almost all of the pastors shook their heads right and left.

Next I would ask: "Dear pastors, do you believe in Jesus?"

They would all yell, "Yes!" in even louder voices.

Finally, I asked: "Is there anyone who has met Jesus and shaken hands with Him?"

As expected, there was no answer. The pastors merely shook their heads right and left.

"If this is so, then in what is your faith grounded," I would ask? "Why is it that you believe in God and Jesus even though you have never seen God nor met Jesus?"

Finally one pastor breaks the silence. Clutching a Bible in his raised right hand, he boldly cries out, "Because of this Bible, I believe!"

Now I ask you, dear reader, this same question: "Are you sure you believe in God or Jesus? In what is your faith grounded?"

None of us have ever seen God, nor met Jesus, nor shaken hands with Him. How then, can we say that we believe in God or Jesus?

Many have heard the Gospel—shared through evangelization—by someone who has believed before them. When one is born-again, often the Holy Spirit moves within the heart and prompts a person to share the Gospel of Jesus Christ. When the Holy Spirit is at work, people like you and me listen. We repent, believe, and confess that Jesus is our Lord and Savior. In every case, it is the moving of the Holy Spirit that leads people to salvation (Rom 10:9–15; John 15:26–27, 16:7–13).

When the Bible is handed to nonbelievers and they are encouraged to believe in God, most turn away. One among thousands chooses to believe in God after reading the Bible. This happens because it is impossible to believe without help from the Holy Spirit. Only the Holy Spirit allows us to recognize sin, (John 16:7–9), guides us into all truth (John 16:13), and testifies to Jesus (John 15:26). No can say, "Jesus is Lord" except by the Holy Spirit (1 Cor 12:3). Incidentally, it was the stirring of the Holy Spirit that prompted followers to write the Bible (2 Tim 3:16; 2 Pet 1:21).

The Holy Spirit plays such a key role in salvation that it is absolutely prudent to ask ourselves how much we know about Him? Without the Holy Spirit, there is no Bible, no Jesus (Son of God), no healing, no resurrection, and no salvation!

It is important to understand that without having the right pneumatology—the understanding of spiritual phenomena—it is extremely difficult to have the right doctrine of God, Christology, Trinity, sin, creation, church, anthropology, soteriology, eschatology, and more.

Unfortunately, many laypersons, ministers, pastors, and even theological professors, do not know much about the Holy Spirit. Without this knowledge, it is easy to treat the Holy Spirit carelessly—or neglect Him altogether. More about this will be explained in chapter 2.

I began attending church in my early teens, but wasn't saved until past the age of forty. In my early thirties, I came to Frankfurt, Germany as the branch manager of a trading company. As in Korea, I attended church zealously, but without having a firm grasp of salvation. While there, I was baptized with the Holy Spirit and saved by the grace of our Lord. Along with this grace came an unquenchable thirst for the Word of God and a burning desire to learn more theology. I enrolled in Chongshin Pastoral Seminary in Sadang-dong, Seoul, Korea, and graduated at the end of winter semester in 2004. I began a ministry for Koreans in Frankfurt although I was over fifty years old.

The subject of my graduate thesis was *A Study of the Work of the Holy Spirit and His Role in the Events of Creation and Salvation*. It was a challenging pursuit that was completed with help and guidance from the Holy Spirit.

This book is a compilation of the thesis, which has been converted into easy-to-understand language, and enhanced with testimonies and illustrations. Some may question man's ability to write about the Holy Spirit. I simply worked to explain what the Holy Spirit revealed to me.

A primary purpose of this book is to encourage all believers to treat the Holy Spirit honorably rather than carelessly; to acknowledge Him as true God (Jer 10:10) and true Lord (2 Cor 3:17–18) rather than neglect Him; and to give thanks, praise, and glory to the Holy Spirit rather than blaspheme Him. In these last days, the wonderful works of salvation and the name of Jesus shall be proclaimed to the ends of the earth—all with the help of the Holy Spirit.

In the end may we all confess, "Holy Spirit, I love you!" just as we confess, "Father, I love you!" or "Jesus, I love you!"

2

Good Morning, Holy Spirit!

It is written, "Their voice has gone out into all the earth, their words to the ends of the world" (Rom 10:18), and "This is the gospel that you heard and that has been proclaimed to every creature under heaven" (Col 1:23). Acts 1:8 demonstrates that these words of Jesus have come to pass:

> But you will receive power when the Holy Spirit comes on you; and you will be my witnesses in Jerusalem, and in all Judea and Samaria, and to the ends of the earth.

The gospel was preached to *the ends of the earth* and *to every creature* long before 100 AD by His disciples who obeyed the Lord's commandment to "Go into all the world and preach the good news to all creation" (Mark 16:15).

In Matthew 24:14, we are told:

> And this gospel of the kingdom will be preached in the whole world as a testimony to all nations, and *then the end will come.*

Obviously, "His coming and the end of the age" (Matt 24:3) has not yet occurred. A more thorough look at Scripture unearths important reasons, including that "the full number of the Gentiles" (Rom 11:25) has not come to salvation and "the number of their fellow servants and brothers who were to be killed" (Rev 6:11) is not yet completed.

Our Lord Jesus, the Son of God, came into this world as flesh and performed many miracles in a three and one-half year period. Before going to heaven, He told his disciples, "I tell you the truth, anyone who has faith in me will do what I have been doing. He will do even greater things than these because I am going to the Father" (John 14:12).

This means that after He (Jesus, the Lord) dies on the cross, comes back to life again, and goes to heaven, He will send the Counselor, which is the Holy Spirit. As Scripture tells us, when the Holy Spirit comes, the disciples will be able to do greater things than the Lord. As promised, the disciples performed many miraculous signs after Pentecost. Collectively, they conducted even more salvation works than Jesus. *The greater things* that Jesus spoke of were the very *salvation of souls* (1 Pet 1:9).

Why has our Lord Jesus not returned though it is the beginning of the twenty-first century and almost 2000 years have passed since His disciples and their disciples carried out these *greater things*? Once again, it is because *the full number of Gentiles* and *the number of fellow servants and brothers to be killed* is yet to be accomplished.

If such greater things had happened continuously from the early church days forward, our Lord Jesus would already have come. It appears that the Holy Spirit chose not to work for reasons that are known only by God.

It is entirely possible that all of us—especially the servants of the Lord—restrict the power of the Holy Spirit. Due to our ignorance of the Holy Spirit who is true God and true Lord, we treat Him carelessly or ignore Him. This is an opinion shared by pastors in the Ukraine and those who attend my seminars in West Africa. However, this is not the opinion held by others.

Headed by puritan John Owen,[1] who is well known as a distinguished seventeenth-century pneumatology scholar, Abraham Kuyper,[2] Sinclair Ferguson,[3] Gordon D. Fee,[4] Arthur W. Pink,[5] Billy Graham,[6] and many other Korean theological scholars, say that churches are ignorant as they treat carelessly, misunderstand, distort, despise, and even blaspheme the Holy Spirit.

A few years ago, on the first Sunday worship of the New Year, I preached a sermon entitled, *Holy Spirit, I Love You!* After the worship service, a male deacon approached and angrily asked, "Dear Pastor! We can say 'God, I love you' or 'Jesus, I love you', but how can we say 'Holy Spirit, I love you?'"

I was speechless with astonishment. I understood that he might be ignorant of the Holy Spirit as he had never attended a Bible study class on pneumatology, but I had not expected him to dishonor the Holy Spirit so blatantly. However, what is certain is that the Holy Spirit is despised at this very moment, not only a few hundred or few thousand years ago.

Do you believe that the Holy Spirit is like us? That He is a person with individual knowledge, His own emotions, and His own will? We will explore this subject a little later. Suppose that you are treated carelessly or despised by other people. How does this make you feel? You probably avoid them and feel uneasy in their presence. Likewise, the Holy Spirit feels grief when He is despised. He feels great sadness

---

1. Owen, *The Holy Spirit*, 29–33.
2. Kuyper, *The Work of the Holy Spirit*, 12, 27.
3. Ferguson, *The Holy Spirit*, 12.
4. Fee, Paul, *The Spirit and the People of God*, vii.
5. Pink, *The Holy Spirit*, 7–8.
6. Graham, *The Holy Spirit*, 8.

when He is not welcomed because He possesses a personality with emotions like us.

A long time ago, the Reverend Benny Hinn wrote the book *Good Morning, Holy Spirit* and it left a deep impression on me. The title indicates simply and without a doubt, that the Holy Spirit is a person! The New Testament clearly specifies that there are three persons in one Godhead, namely the Father, the Son, and the Spirit (Matt 28:19). Similar passages of Scripture confirm that the Holy Spirit, Father, and Son are individual persons with their own knowledge, own emotion, and own will. The following Scriptures yield more evidence in support of this belief:

> But God has revealed it to us by his Spirit. The Spirit searches all things, even the deep things of God. For who among men knows the thoughts of a man except the man's spirit within him? In the same way no one knows the thoughts of God except the Spirit of God. (1 Cor 2:10–11)

This means that the Holy Spirit has perfect knowledge of God.

> And do not grieve the Holy Spirit of God with who you were sealed for the day of redemption. (Eph 4:30)

This means that the Holy Spirit has His own emotion.

> All these are the work of one and the same Spirit, and he gives them to each one, just as he determines. (1 Cor 12:11)

This means that the Holy Spirit has His own will.

Jesus, the Son of God, refers to the Holy Spirit using the third-person pronoun "He" (John 15:26, 16:7–8, 13). In many instances, the Bible speaks of the Holy Spirit as a functioning person. The following scriptural references explain actions in which the Holy Spirit participates:

- "Say, tell" (Acts 8:29, 10:19,13:2; 1 Tim 4:1; Heb 3:7; Rev 2:7)
- "Teach" (John 14:26)
- "Testify" (John 15:26)
- "Encourage" (Acts 9:31)
- "Insist" (Acts 16:6–7)
- "Guide" (John 16:13)
- "Help, intercede" (Rom 8:26–27)

These references demonstrate that the Holy Spirit functions as a person exactly like us. As persons we need to be acknowledged, welcomed, and loved because emotions are a part of our being. Without love and acceptance, we do not feel valued.

Using parallel thought, we begin to understand why the Holy Spirit is willing to work when He is acknowledged and welcomed. Conversely, He will not work yesterday, today, or in the future if He is neglected (1 Sam 2:30b; Isa 63:10–14). All of this, because He is a person!

3

Who Are You, Holy Spirit?

First of all, I would like to explain the meaning of the Holy Spirit. The Holy Spirit is written as *Ruach* in Hebrews in the Old Testament and *Pneuma* in Greek in the New Testament. Both have the same meaning as "breath," "life," "wind," "soul," and "spirit." In the Gospel of John, the description is narrowed to *Parakleto* in Greek, which means "Counselor," "Comforter," "Helper," and "Lawyer." I will explain more about *Parakleto* later.

In English, capital letters are used to designate "the Spirit," "Holy Spirit," "or Holy Ghost." The word "Holy" is regarded with God, illustrating that God is distinguished from worldly things.

Normally, the Trinity is comprised of the "Holy Father, Holy Son, and Holy Spirit" in three persons. There is little objection to uniting all three because the Trinity is absolutely "Holy." However, further scrutiny of the New Testament finds that the "Holy Father" is referenced only one time—in John 17:11. The words "Holy Son" are not used a single time—only "the Son." Discovering the words "Holy Spirit" is easy as this particular two-word name is used many times, which proves the very "holiness" and "purity" of the Holy Spirit.

Next, let us take a look at what the Bible has to say about the Holy Spirit and how He has the equivalent divinity and character of God because the Spirit Himself is God.

We know that "the Lord is everlasting God" (Isa 40:28; Neh 9:5; Rom 16:26). Hebrews 9:14 confirms that the Holy Spirit is also everlasting as it reads, "How much more, then, will the blood of Christ, who through the eternal Spirit offered himself unblemished to God . . . "

We know that "God is mighty or almighty" (Josh 22:22; Ps 50:1; Ezek 10:5). Scripture tells us that "The Holy Spirit will come upon you, and the power of the Most High will overshadow you . . . " (Luke 1:35), which denotes that the Holy Spirit is also almighty, or omnipotent.

We know that "God knows everything" (Josh 22:22; Ps 139:1–4). 1 Corinthians 2:10–11 reinforces this notions as it reads: "But God has revealed it to us by his Spirit. The Spirit searches all things, even the deep thoughts of God. For who among men knows the thoughts of man except man's spirit within him? In the same way no one knows the thoughts of God except the Spirit of God."

This passage also explains that the Holy Spirit knows everything; He is omniscient.

We know that God "fills heaven and earth" (Jer 23:24) through the words, "Where can I go from your Spirit? Where can I flee from your presence" (Ps 139:7)? These words teach that the Spirit is everywhere, or omnipresent.

We know that "God is holy" (Amos 4:2; Isa 6:3) and Romans 1:4 speaks of "the Spirit of holiness," literally "the Spirit is Holy!"

We know that "God is love" (1 John 4:8, 16) and are also told that "the love of the Spirit" (Rom 15:30) and "the fruit of the Spirit is love . . . ," (Gal 5:22) which means the Holy Spirit is love as well.

We know that "God is good" (Ps 118:1), and are told that "you gave your good Spirit to instruct them" (Neh 9:20), which means the Holy Spirit is also good.

We know that "God is gracious" (Exod 34:6; Heb 12:15). In addition, Hebrews 10:29 tells us about "the Spirit of grace," which means that the Holy Spirit is gracious, too.

We know that "God is peace" (Rom 15:13; Heb 13:20) and it is written that "the fruit of the Holy Spirit is peace," (Gal 5:22) which means that the Holy Spirit is also peace.

We know that "God is truth" (Isa 65:16) and John 14:17 speaks of "the Spirit of truth," which means that the Holy Spirit is also truth.

The above Bible verses testify that the Holy Spirit has every character of God and that the Holy Spirit Himself is God. Acts 5:3–4 confirm that the Holy Spirit is God with the use of synonymous words, "lied to the Holy Spirit" and "lied to God."

Now let us examine Scripture for conclusive evidence that the Holy Spirit is "the Lord." 2 Corinthians 3:17–18 says that "The Lord is the Spirit . . . from the Lord, who is the Spirit," which indicates that the Spirit (Holy Spirit) is Lord.

When we call God, "the Lord," of course we mean the Trinity of God—that is the Father, the Son, and the Holy Spirit. They are all God, as is "the Lord." Normally we acknowledge that God, the Father, and God, the Son, are "the Lord" without any objection, but we are miserly to acknowledge that the Holy Spirit is also "the Lord," in spite of the fact that we recognize the Holy Spirit as God.

In the Bible, especially in the New Testament, there are many Scriptures that speak of "the Lord" as "the Holy Spirit." Of course most New Testament references to "the Lord" relate to Jesus, the Son of God, who came to this world in the flesh.

Luke 5:17 states that "the power of the Lord was present for him to heal the sick." In this phrase, "him" means

"Jesus, the Son of God," and "the Lord" means "the Holy Spirit." Matthew 12:28 reinforces that the Holy Spirit is with Jesus, the Son of God, who has driven out demons by the Spirit of God.

Mark 16:20 notes that "the Lord worked with them." In this phrase, "the Lord" means "the Holy Spirit," who is "the Spirit of Jesus" and "the Spirit of the Lord," because Jesus, the Son of God, had already been taken up to heaven and was seated at the right hand of God (Mark 16:19).

In addition, 1 Corinthians 11:23 says, "For I received from the Lord what I also passed on to you. The Lord Jesus, on the night he was betrayed, took bread . . . " Here, the second reference to "the Lord" is definitely "Jesus, the Son of God", whereas the first mention of "the Lord" points to "the Holy Spirit."

In truth, the Apostle Paul has never met Jesus personally, nor has he ever heard any word or teaching directly from Him. Jesus, the Son of God, who was taken up to heaven and seated at the right hand of God, did not reappear and talk to Paul. It was the Holy Spirit or "the Spirit of Jesus Christ" who talked to Paul in a revelation.

The Apostle Paul writes, in Galatians 1:12, that he did not receive it from any man nor was he taught it; rather, he received it by revelation from Jesus Christ. And the God who reveals is not Jesus, but the Holy Spirit because the Holy Spirit is "the Spirit of wisdom and revelation" (Eph 1:17). Therefore, "Jesus Christ" in Galatians 1:12 is not the Son of God but "the Spirit of Jesus Christ."

The words of Acts 1:1–2 speak of the risen Jesus Christ as he instructs the apostles "through the Holy Spirit." Judging from this, Jesus, the Son of God, who sits at the right hand of God, instructs effortlessly "through the Holy Spirit." When Jesus hung on the cross and finished His commission in this world, He said, "it is finished" (John 19:30). He also told His disciples, "when the Counselor, the Spirit of truth comes, He will testify about me (John 15:26) and will teach you all things and will remind you of everything I have said to you" (John 14:26). It is not necessary for Jesus, the Son of God, to come to this world again because He finished His role by providing the way of salvation. The remainder of the salvation work has been handed over to the Holy Spirit. Jesus is now sitting at the right hand of God and is interceding on our behalf.

As we look at the Bible we see that the Holy Spirit spoke predominantly through the mouths of prophets and apostles. For example, "the Holy Spirit spoke through the mouth of David" (Acts 1:16). Often, the Holy Spirit spoke directly to the apostles. This occurs many times in Acts:

- "The Spirit told Philip" (Acts 8:29)
- "The Spirit said to him" (Acts 10:19)
- "The Spirit said" (Acts13:2)
- "The Holy Spirit warns me" (Acts 20:23)
- "The Spirit says" (Acts 21:11)

The Holy Spirit also spoke directly to the prophets in the Old Testament:

> Then the Spirit of the Lord came upon me, and he told me to say . . . (Ezek 11:5)

Just as in many cases in the New Testament, "the Lord" means "the Holy Spirit" and therefore, the Holy Spirit is "the Lord." It is important to accept this overwhelming evidence and remember that the Holy Spirit is a person and He is our God and our Lord.

4

The Holy Spirit and the Trinity

MOST CHURCHGOERS are familiar with the Trinity, although they may not understand it. Some refuse to believe in it because the word "Trinity" is not used in the Bible. Through extensive study of the Bible, however, many theologians conclude that there is "One Godhead consisting of three persons." In an effort to define "One Godhead consisting of three persons" more succinctly, theologians have assigned it the name "Trinity."

An in-depth study of the Bible discloses three persons with the same personality. These three persons are "the Father, the Son, and the Holy Spirit" and they are the same God that makes up One Godhead. The word "Trinity" recognizes this unique union. Several important elements that make up the three-in-one will be explained later.

Theologians and pastors often use word pictures to explain the Trinity. For instance, the substance of the sun is a round shape in the sky. From it comes light and heat, though it is but one sun. Or, note that a car battery generates energy that is used to start the engine and operate the lights. The same energy source created in the battery is drawn on to carry out several functions. Using the same analogy, here is how the Trinity might be taught:

- The Father: God as basic substance
- The Son: God as image
- The Spirit: God as spirit

Although God is omnipresent, some pastors teach that God is distinguished in the field of salvation as follows:

- The Father: God who exists out of the universe
- The Son: God who came into the universe
- The Spirit: God who came into us

Keep in mind that humans, with our severely limited capacity for understanding, will never fully comprehend nor be able to explain the mystery of the Trinity. It is said that the Trinity is the mystery of mysteries and "one of the greatest mysteries of our most holy religion."[1]

As we turn to explore the Trinity, we discover that the Bible yields valuable insight into the Holy Spirit. Promises of a new heaven and a new earth (Isa 65:17, 66:22; 2 Pet 3:13; Rev 21:1), as well as Jesus' role as the bridegroom (John 3:29; 2 Cor 11:2) are found in both the Old and New Testaments. Therefore, as Christians we believe that He will come back as He went into heaven (Acts 1:11) and look forward to "the day of God and speed its coming" (2 Pet 3:12; Rev 22:20).

However, the scene that the Apostle John has seen in heaven is quite different from our expectations. Jesus, the Son of God, after being taken up to heaven, appeared as the image of the Son of Man to deacon Stephen (Acts 7:55–56), to the Apostle John (Rev 1:13–16), and as a rider on a white horse (Rev 19:11–13). The image of the Son of God at the right hand of God's throne is conspicuously absent.

Upon further investigation into the revelation, it is clear that someone is sitting on the throne with the appearance of jasper and carnelian (Rev 4:2–3). The Apostle John saw a Lamb who took the scroll from the right hand of him

---

1. Morgan, G. Campbell, *The Spirit of God*, 44.

who sat on the throne (Rev 5:7). Is the one who sat on the throne the Father but without His whole appearance? In the same scenario, Jesus, the Son of God, is not sitting on the right hand of God the Father as expected.

The Apostle John saw only a Lamb standing in the center of the throne encircled by four living creatures and the elders (Rev 5:6). Just seven verses later, we are told that the one who sits on the throne and the Lamb are present (Rev 5:13). Scripture continues to proclaim that the Lamb is at the center of the throne (Rev 7:17) and states, "the throne of God and of the Lamb" (Rev 22:1, 3), which indicates that God and the Lamb share the same throne.

When Philip said to Jesus, "Lord, show us the Father and that will be enough for us," Jesus answered: "Don't you know me, Philip, even after I have been among you such a long time? Anyone who has seen me has seen the Father. How can you say, 'show us the Father'" (John 14:9–10)? In addition, Jesus Himself said that He and the Father are one (John 10:30). There is no record of the image of the Father or the Son in heaven, but only the Lamb with seven horns and seven eyes (Rev 5:6). Where then, are the Father and Son? If they are one, the Lamb must represent the Father and the Son.

In Isaiah 6:1–9, Isaiah the prophet speaks of observing the Lord, who is King, and the Lord Almighty seated on the throne. He also notes that the train of His robe filled the temple but not his face and that he heard the voice of the Lord. In the New Testament, Luke says "the Lord" is "the Holy Spirit" (Acts 28:25).

The mystery of the Trinity of God is truly amazing, even though it is far beyond our understanding. I would suggest that you believe in the Trinity of God although it is somewhat of a mystery because Scripture overwhelmingly supports it. Personally, it is through the Trinity that I feel the deep love of God.

The Apostle Paul said that the relationship between Christ and the church is a profound mystery much like a husband and wife becoming one flesh (Eph 5:31–32). How can we understand the relationship between Jesus, our bridegroom, and the church, the bride, without comprehending the united relationship between a husband and wife? How can we understand the love between our Father in heaven and a child of God without realizing the love between a parent and child (father and son) in this world? Is it possible that the Lord created a system of family relationships in order that we might experience the love between a parent and child and, therefore, be convinced of the unimaginable love of the Trinity of God? Praise the Lord whose love is incomprehensibly wonderful and great!

The Trinity of God is more clearly revealed in the New Testament (Matt 28:19). Jesus, the Son of God, who was raised from the dead, delivers the great commission to His disciples, saying "Therefore go and make disciples of all nations, baptizing them in the name of the Father and of the Son and of the Holy Spirit . . . . " It is said that there is One Godhead but with three persons—the Father, the Son, and the Holy Spirit. Traditionally, the Holy Spirit is listed as the third person. In numerous scriptures, however, He is named first or second:

- Son Father Spirit (Rom 15:16; 2 Cor 13:13)
- Spirit Son Father (Eph 4:4–6)
- Father Spirit Son (1 Pet 1:2)
- Spirit Father Son (Jude 1:20–21)
- Son Spirit Father (Rom 15:30)

These Scriptures demonstrate that each member of the Trinity of God holds an equal portion in existence, glory, authority, dignity, power and value.

In the Old Testament, persons of the Trinity are not named as specifically as in the New Testament. However, the "Father and Son" concept (not the Father and the Son) is introduced in 2 Samuel 7:14. The words, "you are my Father" (Ps 89:26), "you are our Father" (Isa 63:16, 64:8), and "we have one Father" (Mal 2:10), are examples of this concept. We may think of "the Father" in the Old Testament as simply "the Father as Creator."

In reality, hints of the Trinity are dispersed throughout the Old Testament, starting with Genesis 1:1: "In the beginning, God created the heavens and the earth." In this sentence, God in Hebrew is *Elohim,* which means the plural "gods." From the word *Elohim* we can extrapolate that God in the Trinity created the heavens and the earth. The following scriptural phrases add credence to this argument as they speak in plural terms:

- Let us make man in our image, in our likeness . . . (Gen 1:26)
- The man has now become like one of us . . . (Gen 3:22)
- Come let us go down and confuse their . . . (Gen 11:7)
- And who will go for us? (Isa 6:8)

By using the plural personal pronoun of "us," God indicates that the Trinity of God is working together. Separate persons of the Trinity are designated as "the Spirit of God" (Gen 1:2) and "the image of the Son of God," (Gen 1:27), which agrees with the end of that same passage: "God created man in his own image, in the image of God he created him." Suddenly God uses singular third person pronouns, "he" and "his," while "us" is used in verse 26. "He" in this inference is "the Son of God" who is "the image of the invisible God" (Col 1:15).

We now know that the Trinity of God has been working throughout scripture, from Genesis chapter 1 to Revelation chapter 22. There are additional clues to the workings of the Trinity in the Old Testament. For example, "the Lord" is mentioned three successive times in Numbers 6:24–26, as is "holy" in Isaiah 6:3. Likewise, "the name of the Lord" is written three times in Psalm 113:1–3 and 118:10–12.

Additional evidence is yielded in Isaiah 48:16: "the Sovereign Lord has sent me, with his Spirit." Little imagination is needed to conclude that "the Sovereign Lord" indicates "the Father," "me" is "the image of God as His Son," and "his Spirit" is, of course, "the Holy Spirit.

Isaiah 42:1 states: "Here is my servant, whom I uphold, my chosen one in whom I delight; I will put my Spirit on him" which is also quoted in Matthew 12:8. These prophetic verses speak of Christ, the Messiah, as related to the salvation works of the Trinity of God.

The Lord who is "God in the image of the Son of God" appears many times to Abraham (Gen 17:1, 18:1; John 8:56). to Joshua as "the commander of the Lord" (Joshua 5:13–15) and speaks with Moses on numerous occasions (Exod 33:11; Num 12:8; Deut 34:10).

The salvation work of the Lord might be classified into three different periods:

- The era of God, the Father, who worked during Old Testament times
- The era of Jesus Christ, the Son of God, who worked during His stay in the world;
- The era of the Holy Spirit who has been working since Pentecost.

This breakdown merely points out that the Father worked as the primary body during the Old Testament, Jesus Christ as the main body during His stay in the world, and the Holy Spirit as the predominant body since Pentecost.

It is important to note that during the New Testament, though it appears that Jesus works alone as a Son of Man with His own personality, the Holy Spirit is always with Him and the Father was also in Jesus (John 10:38, 14:10–11, 17:21–23). For example, when John the Baptist baptizes Jesus, the Holy Spirit descends like a dove and a voice is heard from the Father in heaven (Matt 3:16–17; Mark 1:9–11; Luke 3:21–22; John 1:32–34). This scene illustrates dramatically that the Trinity of God works together. I say dramatically because these words are written in all four Gospels, which emphasizes that they are very important.

During the period of the Holy Spirit, initially it seems as if He is working alone, but in truth, He is working with the Father and the Son (John 14:16–23). Jesus, the Son of God, said, "when another Counselor—the Spirit of truth—lives with you" (John 14:16–17) "we (the Son and the Father) will come to him and make our home with him" (John 14:23b). The Holy Spirit is also "the Spirit of the Son" (Gal 4:6) and "the Spirit of the Father" (Matt 10:20). It is impossible to imagine God, the Son, without the Spirit of the Son, and God, the Father, without the Spirit of the Father. Once again we are reminded that the works of salvation and the Trinity of God hold many mysteries.

Now, let us examine several important facts about the three-persons-in-one component of the Trinity of God.

First, each person of the Father, Son, and Holy Spirit is "the Lord" and "God." As explained in the previous chapter, each person is "the Lord our God."

Second, it is important to recognize the *holiness* of each of the three persons. The Trinity of God is nothing if each is not holy. Their holiness is acknowledged when the four living creatures praise and glorify the Lord God Almighty, saying "Holy, holy, holy" (Isa 6:3; Rev 4:8). These creatures are glorifying the holiness of the Father, the Son, and the Holy Spirit.

Third, the Word is tangible evidence that they are three persons in one. "In the beginning was the Word, and the Word was with God, and the Word was God" (John 1:1). Here, God is understood as the Trinity. Further, we are told that "the Word became flesh," which indicates Jesus, the Son of God (John 1:14). In Ephesians 6:17, it is written: "the sword of the Spirit is the word of God." I will explain the relationship between the Holy Spirit and the Word later.

The fourth, fifth, and sixth elements of the three-persons-in-one agreement of the Trinity are their purpose as "Savior," the name of the Trinity of God as "Jesus," and the fact that the Father, the Son, and the Holy Spirit are all "Jesus Christ." I will explain more about the third, fourth, fifth, and sixth points in separate chapters because each is highly significant.

The seventh point is also critical because it allows us to witness the divine immanence of each member of the Trinity. Jesus told His disciples that when the Counselor, the Spirit of truth comes, "we will come to him and make our home with him" (John 14:16–23). When the Counselor comes to each one of us, we—the Father and the Son (Jesus)—will also come to him and dwell with him. The indwelling of the Holy Spirit means that the Trinity of God is dwelling within us.

For this reason the Apostle Paul said, "it is God who works in you" (Phil 2:13), "Jesus Christ is in you" (Rom 8:10; 2 Cor 13:5; Col 1:27), and "Christ lives in me" (Gal 2:20).

As indicated previously in this chapter, the most important substance of the three-persons-in-one union is "the Holy Spirit."

The words "God is Spirit" are written in John 4:24 in both the New International Version and the New King James Version of the Bible. To say, "the Spirit is God," sounds absolutely right, but to say, "God is Spirit," does not sound logical. In the Greek Bible, this sentence is arranged to emphasize that God is a spiritual being, which means the Father and the Son are also spiritual beings as well as the Holy Spirit.

Incidentally, can you imagine God the Father without the Holy Spirit who is also "the Spirit of the Father?" Can you envision the Son of God without the Holy Spirit who is also "the Spirit of the Son?"

The Trinity can be explained more easily using an apple tree as an analogy. An apple tree has its own roots, branches, stems, leaves, flowers, and fruit. Each may be a different shape or color, but all have one common feature, the apple, and the sap of the apple consists of DNA. The same logic can be applied to the Trinity of God. It exists in three different persons and each has a different purpose but also has common features that make them one. The most important common denominator is the Holy Spirit. As mentioned before, when the Holy Spirit dwells in us, the Father and the Son also reside in us. Stated more directly, when the Father and the Son dwell within us—God is in us and Christ is in us.

Arthur Pink states in his book *The Holy Spirit*:

> The essential, vital, central element in the life of the soul and the work of the church is the Person of the Spirit.[2]

In his book *Keep In Step With The Spirit*, theologian James Packer adds these thoughts:

> First, the New Testament's Christ-centered view of the ministry of the Holy Spirit needs to be recovered and As knowing the Holy Spirit means precisely knowing Christ, so honoring the Holy Spirit means precisely honoring Christ.[3]

---

2. Pink, *The Holy Spirit*, 7.
3. Packer, *Keep in Step With the Spirit*, 241, 260.

The words "God is Spirit" emphasize that God is unlimited in space (omnipresence), time (forever), power (omnipotence), knowledge (omniscience), wisdom, glory, forgiveness, and love. All of these qualities are of the Spirit because the Spirit cannot be limited. For example, Jesus, the Son of God, was limited. When He was in Jerusalem, He could not be in Bethlehem because He was in the flesh. Of course, we believe that Jesus is also God and unlimited in space because the Spirit of Jesus, or Spirit of the Son, was with Him and the Spirit of the Son is unlimited. Ephesians 3:18 paints a beautiful picture of the unlimited depths of Christ's love as it reads: "to grasp how wide and long and high and deep is the love of Christ." Love without limit is made possible because "God is Spirit" and the Spirit is unlimited.

Furthermore, "God is Spirit," indicates that "God is invisible" (Col 1:15; 1 Tim 1:17; Heb 11:27). Scripture reinforces this conclusion through the words: "no one has ever seen or can see God" (John 1:18; 1 Tim 6:16; 1 John 4:12) and "no one may see God and live" (Gen 32:30; Exod 33:20; Deut 5:24; Judg 13:22). The Spirit is essentially invisible!

Lastly, it is important to recognize that "God is Spirit" underscores that God without the Spirit is God no more in the same way that man without the spirit is man no more since "the body without the spirit is dead" (Jas 2:26). Therefore, the most basic element making up the three-persons-in-one is "the Holy Spirit!"

In the beginning of this chapter, I mentioned that the word "Trinity" is not written in the Bible, yet the Bible has proved that the three are one. It should be noted, however, that some English and German Bible translations use the words "three are one" as follows:

> For there are three who bear witness in heaven:
> the Father, the Word, and the Holy Spirit; and
> these three are one. (NKJV, 1 John 5:7)

The Luther version (*Martin Luther Uebersetzung*) used officially by German churches (*Evangelische Kirche in Deutschland, EKD*) displays the verse as:

> *Denn drei sind's, die da Zeugnis geben im Himmel:
> der Vater, das Wort und der Heilige Geist; und
> diese drei sind eins.*

The Schlachter version 2000 (*Schlachter Uebersetzung, Das Neue Testament*), which is used by many free churches reads:

> *Denn drei sind es, die Zeugnis ablegen im Himmel:
> der Vater, das Wort und der Heilige Geist, und
> diese drei sind eins.*

The meaning of these German versions is identical to the NKJV. Since the Word is Jesus, the Son of God who came to this world with flesh, it is clearly written that there are three (the Father, the Son, and the Spirit) who bear witness in heaven that "Jesus is Christ" and these three persons are one! The German word for "Trinity" is *Dreieinigkeit,* "three are one" as it stands.

I do not know why such key words were deleted or translated differently in various manuscripts of the Bible, and we are taught that an original text of the Bible does not exist. I believe that God would not have let the original Word of Life be lost and that it is hidden somewhere in the world. But, I will leave this matter to the experts as I am sure the truth will be disclosed in due time.

As we return to study the Holy Spirit, let me reiterate that each person of the Trinity of God is equal in every respect. In fact, each respects and honors one another, according to the Bible as it states that the Father and the Son glorify each other (John 5:19–23, 12:28, 13:20, 17:1–5; 2 Pet 1:17). We are also told that the Spirit brings glory to the Son (John 16:14). On the other hand, on many occasions, the Son glorifies the Holy Spirit, too.

There is a story that Jesus healed a demon-possessed man (Mark 5:1–20; Luke 8:26–39). The man went into town and told everyone how much Jesus had done for him. But Jesus actually asked him to tell them how much *the Lord* has done for him (Mark 5:19), or how much *God* has done for him (Luke 8:39), rather than Jesus Himself. Of course we know that Jesus is "Lord" and "God" but He always humbles Himself by declaring that he is "the Son of Man." Jesus made this distinction in identity because He recognized that "the Spirit of God" drove out demons (Matt 12:28). This is His way of signifying that "the Holy Spirit" is, in truth, "Lord" and "God."

Jesus said, "Anyone who speaks a word against the Son of Man will be forgiven, but anyone who speaks against the Holy Spirit will not be forgiven, either in this age or in the age to come" (Matt 12:31–32). He also states that all of His ministries and works can be done only after "the Spirit of the Lord" comes into Him and anoints Him (Luke 4:18). It is interesting to note that Jesus said "the Spirit of the Lord" instead of "the Holy Spirit" or simply "the Spirit." The choice of words is significant because "the Spirit of the Lord" means "the Spirit who is the Lord" or "the Spirit who works as the Lord." In this way, Jesus exalts the Spirit! A more thorough examination of related word choices is undertaken in chapter 5, *Other Titles of the Holy Spirit.*

In Isaiah 61:1, Luke uses the words, "the Spirit of the Sovereign Lord." The Prophet Isaiah describes the Spirit as "the Sovereign Lord" who rules over the heavens and the earth (Acts 4:24; Rev 6:10). What a mysterious, yet graceful figure this Trinity of God!

For this reason, it is wise for us to call upon "the Lord" or "God" within the exact context of His name while worshiping because the Father, the Son, and the Spirit are all Lord and God. Although "the Lord" and "God" are part of the Trinity, when we keep the Holy Spirit in mind during worship and praise, we free this person of the Trinity to perform even more wonderful works. The Father is in heaven and the Son is sitting at the right hand of the throne, but it is actually "the Holy Spirit" who is Lord, the God, who is accepting our worship, moving within our hearts, making fellowship, and communicating among us now in this place.

Please do not misunderstand that we worship only to the Holy Spirit. The Father and the Son are together within the Holy Spirit who is the Spirit of the Father and the Son. "The Name of Jesus" is within them and "Jesus" is "the Name of the Trinity of God." If we call upon the Name of Jesus, it is the same as when we call upon the Trinity of God. Many miraculous signs will occur when we call upon the Name of Jesus since His Name is synonymous with salvation. Therefore, we worship, praise, glorify, exalt, and love the Name of Jesus forever!

5

Other Titles of the Holy Spirit

THERE ARE lots of titles attributed to the Holy Spirit in the Bible, including "the Spirit of God" (Gen 1:2), "the Spirit of the Lord" (Judg 3:10), "God's Spirit" (1 Cor 3:16), "the Spirit of Christ" (1 Pet 1:11), "the Spirit of Jesus" (Acts 16:7), "the Spirit of truth" (John 14:17), "the Spirit of holiness" (Rom 1:4), "the Spirit of wisdom" (Deut 34:9), "the Spirit of wisdom and revelation" (Eph 1:17), "the Spirit of his Son" (Gal 4:6), "the Spirit of Jesus Christ" (Phil 1:19), "the Spirit of sonship" (Rom 8:15), "the Spirit of glory and of God" (1 Peter 4:14), "the good Spirit" (Neh 9:20), "the eternal Spirit" (Heb 9:14), "the Spirit of grace" (Heb 10:29), "the Spirit of your Father" (Matt 10:20), "the Spirit of life" (Rom 8:2), and "the Spirit of our God" (1 Cor 6:11).

Why do you think the Holy Spirit is expressed in so many different ways when it is appropriate to simply call Him "the Spirit" or "the Holy Spirit?" The reason is that each title illustrates another side of the personality, character, and substance of the Holy Spirit. Each name also lists His various works.

For example, "the Spirit of God" means that the Holy Spirit is "God" and that He is "doing God's work as God." Likewise "the Spirit of the Lord" confirms that the Spirit is "the Lord" and that He is working as "the Lord." "The

Spirit of Jesus Christ" deems that the Spirit is "Jesus Christ" who is working as "Jesus Christ" and with the personality, character, and substance of "Jesus Christ."

In English grammar, when two nouns appear on both sides of the preposition "of," both nouns are appositive, or equal. For example, if we say "the city of Seoul," Seoul means the city and the name of the city is Seoul, which means that "Seoul" and "the city" are equal. Likewise "the Spirit of Christ," "the Spirit of the Father," "the Spirit of the Son," and "the Spirit of truth," etc. can be explained in the same manner.

In his book *The Holy Spirit*, author John Owen writes accurately:

> He is called, by way of eminence, the Holy Spirit. This appellation is very frequent both in the Old and New Testament and he is so called from his sanctifying us, or making us holy.[1]

The words "eternal Spirit" (Heb 9:14) announce that the character of the Holy Spirit is eternal and the words "Spirit of grace" (Heb 10:29) denote the graceful character of the Holy Spirit.

In addition to traditional names, such as "the Spirit" or "the Holy Spirit," His name is uttered in numerous other expressions:

- the breath of the Almighty (Job 32:8)
- the breath of God (Job 27:3)
- the breath of God's mouth (Job15:30)

Actually, breath belongs to the Holy Spirit and the Holy Spirit controls breath, which means the Holy Spirit possesses the power to control life and death (Ps 104:29–30; Isa 42:5; Acts 17:25). The definition of "spirit" in English

---

1. Owen, *The Holy Spirit*, 57.

is derived from "*ruach*" in Hebrew and "*pneuma*" in Greek, and both translate as "breath, wind, and spirit."

"Hand," "finger," and "arm" are frequently used to describe the Holy Spirit because they emphasize aspects of His power. Supporting references can be found in the following Scriptures:

- the hand of the Lord (Isa 25:10; Ezek 1:3)
- God's hand (1 Sam 5:11)
- his holy arm (Isa 52:10)
- your mighty hand (2 Chr 6:32)
- the work of your fingers, or hands (Ps 8:3, 6)

Luke 11:20 says, "But if I drive out demons by the finger of God, then the kingdom of God has come to you," and the parallel phrase of Jesus' lesson is written in Matthew as "the Spirit of God" (Matt 12:28).

In 1 Chronicles 28:12, we read: "He gave him the plans of all that the Spirit had put in his mind for the courts of the temple of the Lord and all the surrounding rooms." A few verses later, the dialogue picks up with, "All this," David said, "I have in writing from the hand of the Lord upon me, and he gave me understanding in all the details of the plan" (1 Chr 28:19).

King David expressed "the hand of the Lord" as "the Spirit."

The following expressions can also be found:

- the eyes of the Lord (Deut 11:12; 1 Kgs 15:26; 2 Chr 16:9; Prov 5:21)
- your eyes (1 Kgs 8:29; 2 Chr 6:40; Neh 1:6)
- my eyes (1 Kgs 11:38; Jer 16:17)

In relation to the above words, the Apostle John saw a Lamb with "seven eyes" (Rev 5:6), which represent "the seven spirits of God" that were sent out into all the earth.

Revelation 3:1 says that Jesus holds "seven spirits of God." This verse does not mean that there are seven Spirits, but rather that the Holy Spirit has perfect and full power because the number seven is represented as perfect in the Bible. To translate, "the eyes of the Lord" means "the Holy Spirit" who searches and judges not only the world but also all of the thoughts and attitudes of my heart. (Heb 4:12–13) Scripture supports this thought process as it is written: "where can I go from your Spirit? Where can I flee from your presence" (Ps 139:7)?

Now I would like to share the testimony of one Korean pastor. Early one summer in the twentieth century, the young evangelist worked in a small Korean village where typhoid fever prevailed. One church member was taken ill and died. Owing to poor medical prevention and treatment methods, when anyone died of the epidemic, apart from paying a console visit, the dead were buried immediately—without a funeral ceremony—in order to prevent infection.

The young evangelist, however, had visited this particular man's house, worshipped there, and arranged for a funeral service. Soon after, the evangelist also was taken ill and died. He remained in the coffin for nine hours and then awoke. The pastor testifies that he was taken up to heaven during this time.

An angel took him before the throne of God where he saw a big white screen over the throne. Everything he did by his mouth, hands, heart, and mind during his entire life was projected onto the screen. An archangel told the Lord that he should be thrown into hell, but the Lord instructed the archangel to send the man back to earth because he had something more to do in the world.

The one thing he could not forget about heaven is that he saw four living creatures around the throne that were covered front to back with video camera lenses. While I was listening to the testimony, I suddenly became convinced that our Lord is taking pictures of everything I say, do, and think. I became fearful and began to tremble.

In a vision, the Apostle John explains that he saw four creatures covered with eyes, in front and in back (Rev 4:6, 8) and the prophet Ezekiel writes the same (Ezek 10:12). The video camera had not been invented in biblical times. Is this not "the eyes of the Holy Spirit" who "searches the heart and examines the mind" (Jer 17:10, 20:12)? It is possible that Old Testament scenarios, such as "the eyes like flaming torches" as shown to the Prophet Daniel (Dan 10:6) and, "the eyes like blazing fire" shown to the Apostle John (Rev 1:14, 2:18, 19:12) might be similarly related.

We have to understand the real intention of the Holy Spirit, the author of the Bible (Isa 34:16; 2 Tim 3:16; 2 Pet 1:21), and why He has written "the Spirit" or "the Holy Spirit" instead of simply "the Lord" or "God." Since God created everything, why has He written lots of different titles that include descriptions of the Holy Spirit? I propose that the Holy Spirit uses a wide array of titles to convey, "Actually, I have done everything!"

As mentioned before, the Trinity of God has worked and continues to work together since the beginning, but the Bible testifies that the Spirit has actually done much of the work and remains to finalize God's plan.

Even though the Spirit wrote the Bible through many different prophets, it is quite clear that the Bible was written with the full knowledge of the Father and the Son. The Spirit who searches all things, even the deep things of God, wrote the Bible with acknowledgement and agreement of the Father and the Son, because "the Holy Spirit" is "the Spirit of the Father" (Matt 10:20) and also "the Spirit of the Son" (Gal 4:6).

Renowned American theologian Arthur Pink said in his book *The Holy Spirit*:

> By means of them, God spells out Himself to us, sometimes by one of His perfections, sometimes by another. What has been said above serves to indicate the importance of the present aspect of our subject. What the Holy Spirit is in His Divine person and ineffable character is made known unto us by means of the many names and varied titles which are accorded to Him in Holy Writ.[2]

---

2. Pink, *The Holy Spirit*, 16.

6

The Symbols of the Holy Spirit

THERE ARE various symbols in the Bible regarding the Holy Spirit. Some may be familiar, such as the dove (Matt 3:16), oil (Acts 10:38), water (John 7:38–39), fire (Acts 2:3–4), and wind (John 3:8). Let us examine the reasons these symbols—especially water, fire, and wind—are used in the Bible.

First, water, fire, and wind equal life. All living beings cannot live without water, fire (light and heat), and wind (breath). These symbols demonstrate that the Holy Spirit controls life itself (Rom 8:2).

Second, water, fire, and wind represent cleanliness. At least one of these elements is required to clean anything that is dirty. These symbols reinforce the principle that the Holy Spirit, who is also "the Spirit of Holiness" (Rom 1:4), controls cleanliness and purifies mankind to make him holy.

Third, water, fire, and wind create power. This power is at work today in the form of heavy rains, floods, waterfalls, tsunamis (water); massive forest fires, oil field fires, bombs of all kinds (fire); and typhoons, tornados, and hurricanes (wind). These symbols demonstrate that the Holy Spirit manages all earthly powers.

Fourth, water, fire, and wind stand for judgment, namely "judgment of death." At the time of Noah, the whole world was judged by water. At present, many places in the world are judged partially by water, wind, and fire. The Lord's ongoing judgment is confirmed as we are told, "I bring prosperity and create disaster; I, the Lord, do all these things" (Isa 45:7) and "The Lord works out everything for his own ends—even the wicked for a day of disaster" (Prov 16:4).

The Last Judgment will be made by fire (Isa 4:4; 2 Pet 3:7). Here, breath (wind) is taken away from all living beings and therefore, we will die. This symbolizes that the Holy Spirit manages the ultimate judgment of mankind.

Through these symbols, it is important to understand that life and death depend on the Holy Spirit who has the sovereign power of God over all generations. So that more souls can be saved for eternity, churches must honor, respect, and rely on the Holy Spirit so that they can accomplish all salvation works as soon as possible.

7

The Holy Spirit and Creation

IN PREVIOUS chapters we discussed that all works of creation and salvation are carried out through the teamwork of the Trinity of God. In Genesis 1:1 it is written: "In the beginning God created the heavens and the earth." *Ellohim*, the plural for "God" in Hebrew, tells us that the Trinity of God will work together until the very last paragraph of Revelation is fulfilled. I have also stated that all of the work was, and continues to be, carried out by the person of the Holy Spirit.

Of course the Bible does not say that the Holy Spirit alone created *nothing* into *being*. The Trinity of God works together with each person fulfilling different roles. The Holy Spirit works as the performer of the *will* of God as expressed by the *Word* of God, and the Holy Spirit converts *disorder* to *order*. The Holy Spirit's role in creation is laid before us in a series of scriptural passages.

> Now the earth was formless and empty, darkness was over the surface of the deep, and the Spirit of God was hovering over the waters. (Gen 1:2)

We have to understand God's intention for writing "the Spirit of God" in verse 2 whereas it is enough for Him to write only "God" in verse 1. Once again, God is differentiating between persons of the Trinity and indicating that the Holy Spirit carries out His instructions.

> By the word of the Lord were the heavens made, their starry host by the breath of his mouth. (Ps 33:6)

Along with the heavens, "countless stars of the sky" (Jer 33:22) and the earth as it exists today, are personal products of the Holy Spirit.

> When you send your Spirit, they are created, and you renew the face of the earth. (Ps 104:30)

> The grass withers and the flowers fall, because the breath of the Lord blows on them. (Isa 40:7)

As stated above, the Holy Spirit controls the creation and preservation of everything in heaven and on earth.

> The Lord God formed the man from the dust of the ground and breathed into his nostrils the breath of life and the man became a living being. (Gen 2:7)

> The Spirit of God has made me; the breath of the Almighty gives me life. (Job 33:4)

As shown in these Old Testament passages, the Holy Spirit controls life and death, the blessing and curse of humankind. He even makes a vast living army from dried bones (Ezekiel 37:1–13).

Many other theologians speak similarly regarding the Holy Spirit and creation. Arthur Pink states:

> The works ascribed to the Spirit clearly demonstrate His Godhead. Creation itself is attributed to Him, no less than to the Father and the Son.[1]

John Owen adds:

> Whereas the order of operation among the distinct persons, depends on the order of their subsistence; the concluding, completing and perfecting acts are ascribed to the Holy Ghost. And the finishing of all these works is ascribed to the Holy Ghost.[2]

Hendrikus Berkhof continues:

> Therefore, I would propose this preliminary definition of the Spirit: It is God's inspiring breath by which he grants life in creation and re-creation. . . . God's Spirit is God acting.[3]

Be rest assured that the Holy Spirit is personally and directly involved in completing the creation of heaven and earth, and everything in it!

---

1. Pink, *The Holy Spirit*, 15.
2. Owen, *The Holy Spirit*, 78.
3. Berkhof, *The Doctrine of the Holy Spirit*, 14.

8

The Holy Spirit and Salvation

Now let us look at the role the Holy Spirit plays in salvation. His contribution is paramount because He is the one who performed the works of creation and preservation and who is now active in the works of salvation.

Saints who believe in Jesus acknowledge that all sixty-six books of the Bible are correct and without error, and that the smallest letter and the least stroke of a pen will be accomplished (Matt 5:18). However, that doesn't stop us from asking "Why?" when we read confusing, or even troubling, portions of the Word. I would suggest that is it hard to understand the intention of God, the Spirit, who is the writer of the Bible, unless we determine to answer the question: "What is His purpose in writing the Bible?"

Readers frequently ask, "Why did God create the heavens and the earth?" "Why is the blood of animals shed?" "Why did God send His Son to this world?" "Why has He sent the Holy Spirit to us?" Look closely. Every one of these questions relates to salvation! If we were asked to select just one word from all sixty-six books of the Old and the New Testaments, it would have to be "Jesus," which means "God is salvation."

In the Greek, "Jesus" is translated from the Hebrew *Joshua,* which literally translates as "Jehovah (*Yahweh*) is salvation," or "God is salvation." The following Scripture references support this argument:

- For God so loved the world that he gave his one and only Son, that whoever believes in him shall not perish but have eternal life. (John 3:16)
- Believe in the Lord Jesus, and you will be saved—you and your household. (Acts 16:31)
- For you are receiving the goal of your faith, the salvation of your souls. (1 Pet 1:9)

The words above are merely a brief example; the Bible talks about salvation continuously.

Jesus Himself, the Son of God, said, "For the Son of Man came to seek and to save what was lost" (Luke 19:10).

Since the creation of the world, all the works of the Trinity of God have been progressing toward a purpose and that purpose is salvation, which will be carried out to its completion until the day of Christ Jesus (Phil 1:6).

The works of salvation, as well as the works of creation and preservation, are the teamwork of the Trinity of God. It is utterly impossible to perform the works of salvation without all members of the Trinity—the Father, the Son, and the Holy Spirit. Ephesians 1:3–4 says, "the God and Father of our Lord chose us in him before the creation of the world." From this, it is clear that we cannot be saved unless the Father has chosen us. However, there is neither redemption nor forgiveness of sins without the blood of Jesus (Eph 1:7). If there is no forgiveness of sins, of course, salvation is impossible. Still, this is not enough. We must believe.

The Bible says, "For it is with your heart that you believe and are justified, and it is with your mouth that you confess and are saved" (Rom 10:10). However, "a seal, the promised Holy Spirit, who is a deposit guaranteeing our inheritance" (Eph 1:13–14) is only offered if our faith and

The Holy Spirit and Salvation 41

confession is true and appropriate against God's standard. The Holy Spirit's seal is required for salvation.

In real-world terms, I offer a personal example. Say I want to go to the United States with my Korean passport. But the U.S. government will not approve a visa if I only offer my wish to go to the United States. I am required to file a visa application to the embassy or consulate of the United States. But, the government does not issue visas simply by receiving a filled out application. Regardless of whether I am wealthy, a famous professor, a four-star general, or a spiritually powerful pastor, I will qualify for a visa only if the contents written on my visa application are suitable according to the laws of the U.S. government.

Likewise, we have to fulfill the law of the Kingdom of God if we want to go to the Kingdom of God, and that law is *believing in Jesus*. The same principle applies with my visa application to the U.S. government. If I say I believe in Jesus, only the Father in heaven can judge whether my faith in Jesus is right or wrong. Only after my faith is accepted by the Father does He send the Holy Spirit to guarantee my deposit, which in the Bible is referred to as "sealing with the Holy Spirit" (2 Cor 1:22). Only the seal of the Holy Spirit is the deposit guaranteeing that I am going to the Kingdom of God and that the salvation of my soul is complete.

In relation to this, I feel compelled to discuss the familiar "prayer for reception" or "sinner's prayer." After the Gospel is shared by individual evangelists, delivered in worship, or presented at revivals, the preacher often invites nonbelievers to accept Jesus Christ as their personal Lord and Savior. He asks that a "prayer for reception" be recited. Each nonbeliever who decides to believe in Jesus is asked to confess that he is a sinner and that he now believes that Jesus was sent to this world in the flesh, shed His blood on the cross, died, was raised from the dead, taken up to heaven, and will come again. Once this prayer is offered, the minister declares that the new believer is now saved. The Bible tells us that anyone who wants to be saved must confess such a "prayer for reception." However, it is illogical that a person who confesses the "prayer for reception" is suddenly saved.

In my teens, I confessed Jesus as my personal Lord and Savior, and was baptized by my senior pastor. After several decades I came to Germany and, as in Korea, attended Korean church zealously. One day a young woman who was a deacon came to me with a serious look and asked: "Deacon Kim, are you sure of your salvation?" ("Sure of salvation" means that if you die today, you are sure to go to heaven.)

I was at a loss in how to answer and got angry because of her impertinent attitude. I shouted back, "How do I know whether I am saved or not! It depends on God!"

As a deacon, I was embarrassed that she had asked me such a question. If I had been sure of my salvation, I might have said, "Amen! Hallelujah!" Unfortunately, I was not saved at that time. When I learned there was a way to guarantee salvation, I was so grateful to God. Being baptized by the Holy Spirit allowed me to have definite faith in my salvation.

It is possible to be born again with the Holy Spirit as soon as we are baptized with water, or confess our faith earnestly and wholeheartedly. However, a large number of people simply attend church on the supposition or misunderstanding that they are saved. Please refer to chapter 11, "The Holy Spirit and Baptism" for a thorough explanation of what it takes to be baptized by (or with) the Holy Spirit.

The oceans containing approximately four percent salt are never going to spoil. "You are the salt of the earth," said our Lord Jesus, but shouldn't we—the churches—examine ourselves as to whether we are salt or have lost our saltiness?

Sometimes pastors insist that when a person confesses "Jesus as Lord," he or she receives the Holy Spirit and is saved. This conclusion is drawn from reading 1 Corinthians 12:3: "no one can say, 'Jesus is Lord,' except by the Holy Spirit." Anyone who is born again by the Holy Spirit has definitely confessed that Jesus is Lord, but just because one confesses this does not mean they are born again with the Holy Spirit. For example, to say that a "horse is an animal" is correct, but to state that all "animals are horses" is wrong. This reasoning is behind Jesus, the Son of God's statement, "Not everyone who says to me, 'Lord, Lord,' will enter the kingdom of heaven" (Matt 7:21).

Now let us look historically at the Trinity of God and salvation. As explained previously, the work of salvation is shared amongst the Father, the Son, and the Holy Spirit. Without any one of them, salvation would be impossible. In the Old Testament, the Father was the primary body; the Son was the main body in the New Testament; and since Pentecost, the Holy Spirit has been the main host through the churches in order to accomplish salvation. These days are generally referred to as "the era of the Spirit" or "the era of the church" since Pentecost.

The Father, God, tells us that we must believe in Jesus, His Son, if we want to go to the kingdom of heaven (John 3:16; Acts 16:31). No one can go to heaven unless he believes in Jesus. There is no other name under heaven given to men by which we must be saved (Acts 4:12).

Jesus also said, "I am the way and the truth and the life. No one comes to the Father except through me" (John 14:6). Jesus is the very "Way" that leads all people on earth to the kingdom of heaven. This is possible only through Jesus, the Son of God, who is "true man" as well as "true God." The Father said to Peter, James, and John who went up to the high mountain with Jesus, "This is my Son, whom I love; with him I am well pleased. Listen to him" (Matt 17:5; Mark 9:7; Luke 9:35)! God asks them to listen to Jesus only, not Moses or Elijah. At that time many people, including the disciples of Jesus, were beginning to think that Jesus was a prophet similar to Moses and Elijah.

After that, Jesus spoke through the Apostle John, saying no one can enter the Kingdom of God unless he is born of water and the Spirit. Shortly before He was crucified, Jesus taught His disciples continuously regarding the Counselor, the Spirit of truth (John 14–16), and encouraged them to "receive the Holy Spirit" after He was resurrected (John 20:22).

After his blood was shed on the cross for the redemption of our sins and He had finished His ministry on earth, Jesus said, "It is finished" (John 19:30). Jesus knew it was impossible for His beloved disciples to enter the Kingdom of God without receiving the Holy Spirit, so He commanded them not to leave Jerusalem until they received the Holy Spirit (Luke 24:49; Acts 1:4–5). According to Jesus there is no other way to enter the kingdom of heaven but to receive the Holy Spirit.

Since no one among us has seen our Father in heaven or met Jesus, who came to this world 2000 years ago and now resides with the Father, how can we believe in God or Jesus? How can we claim them as the foundation of our faith? Only the Holy Spirit can guide us into all truth (John 16:13). Only the Holy Spirit can convict the world of guilt (John 16:7–9). Only can we enter into the Kingdom of God after being born again with the Holy Spirit (John 3:5).

Only the Holy Spirit can testify to the authenticity of Jesus (John 15:26). The Holy Spirit says that Jesus is the Son of God who came to this world with flesh, shed blood and died on the cross for the redemption of our sins, was raised from the dead three days later, ascended into heaven, and will come again one day soon. You and I can only go to heaven if we "believe in the name of Jesus" (John 3:16–18, 6:40, 11:25–26; 14:26).

It is important that believers acknowledge not only that the Holy Spirit is completing works of creation and preservation, but also works of salvation. The heroes of the cross and Pentecost, two of the highest peaks of the works of salvation in the era of the New Testament, are, of course, the Son of God and the Holy Spirit. It is vital to note the close connection between the cross and Pentecost. Pentecost was possible only because of the cross, and the crucifixion is meaningless without Pentecost. Pentecost was accomplished through Jesus who died on the cross, rose from the dead, and was taken up to heaven. It was the completion of His ministry— especially the resurrection—that was done with the help of the Holy Spirit. The following is a list of ministries the Holy Spirit carried out through the lifetime of Jesus Christ, the Son of God:

- conceived and born through the Holy Spirit
(Matt 1:18; Luke 1:35)
- when baptized with water by John the Baptist, the Holy Spirit came down to Jesus
(Matt 3:16; Mark 1:10; Luke 3:22; John 1:32)
- the Spirit sent Jesus out into the desert"
(Mark 1:12; Luke 4:1–2)
- Jesus returned to Galilee in the power of the Spirit
(Luke 4:14)
- the ministries of Jesus are by the Spirit of the Lord"(Luke 4:18–19)
- Jesus drove out demons by the Spirit of God
(Matt 12:28; Luke 11:20)
- Jesus shed the blood and offered himself through the eternal Spirit (Heb 9:14)
- the Spirit raised Jesus from the dead (Rom 8:11)

- Jesus gave instructions through the Holy Spirit to the apostles (Acts 1:2)

The Holy Spirit then came down at the wonderful event of Pentecost and from that time forward, the Holy Spirit *alone* has been completing the works of salvation. I use the word "alone" to distinguish the Holy Spirit who is also a perfect person—whole and complete on His own. The Father and the Son are with the Holy Spirit. This is part of the mystery of the Trinity of God, too, is it not?

Jesus knew that the role of the Holy Spirit was critical for the works of salvation. For this reason, he said, "every sin and blasphemy will be forgiven men, but the blasphemy against the Spirit will not be forgiven. Anyone who speaks a word against the Son of Man will be forgiven, but anyone who speaks against the Holy Spirit will not be forgiven, either in this age or in the age to come" (Matt 12:31–32; Mark 3:28–29). When someone does not believe in Jesus after receiving the message of an evangelist who is guided and moved by the Holy Spirit, he can never be saved because a sinner cannot enter the kingdom of heaven. To not believe in Jesus is sin (John 16:9).

The following parable helps to clarify this point. In a certain country in Africa, many people are starving due to a long drought, and the U.S. government is sending lots of rice to that country as aid. That government announces on the air:

"Dear people, the U.S. government has sent lots of rice for our people! Anyone who runs short of food can come and take as much rice as they need! It is free; you don't need to pay any money! Please, come and rescue yourself!"

When the people hear this announcement, those who believe the word come and take the rice, saving their lives. However, the people who do not believe the word do not come and they starve to death. First, they are starving to death because they have no food, now they are starving to death because they do not believe the word. This is the same principle as first they are going to hell because of their sins (sinners) and now they are going to hell because they do not believe in Jesus Christ.

Let us look at the word of God in John 1:12:

> Yet to all who received him, to those who believed in his name, he gave the right to become children of God.

Namely, "to believe in Jesus" means "to believe in his name," which also means, "to receive him." In doing so, we have the right to become children of God. Once we become children of God, we can enter the Kingdom of God and this is salvation.

Now, let us explore the word "receive" and how it ties in to salvation.

What does "to receive Jesus" really mean? How can we receive Jesus today, since He came to this world in the flesh, died, and was taken up to heaven 2000 years ago? I will tell you the conclusion in advance. To receive Jesus means that I receive, in my heart, the Holy Spirit, Counselor, who comes in the name of Jesus.

Before finishing His works in this world, Jesus told His disciples many times about the Counselor (John 14, 16). Jesus said that when He goes to the Father, the Counselor, who is the Spirit of truth, would come and be with us forever. And this Counselor is the one who speaks to the Father in our defense, "Jesus Christ, the Righteous One" (1 John 2:1). He repeatedly said:

> I will not leave you as orphans; I will come to you. Before long, the world will not see me anymore, but you will see me. Because I live, you also will live. On that day you will realize that I

am in my Father, and you are in me, and I am in you." (John 14:18–20) He adds, "after a little while you will see me," (John 16:16) and "I will see you again. (John 16:22)

The Greek word for "receive" is *lambano* and it is used in John 20:22, Acts 10:47, and Acts 19:2. Once again, "to believe in Jesus" is "to believe in Jesus' name" and "to receive Jesus" is "to receive the Holy Spirit, the Counselor."

If we believe and confess wholeheartedly, we will receive the Holy Spirit, the Counselor, immediately. Some may ask, "What do I have to do, to believe in Jesus Christ or to receive the Holy Spirit in order to be saved?" These questions are one and the same, much like receiving both sides of a coin or the palm and back of a hand. Another example might be to compare water temperature with the boiling point. Suppose we would like to kill bacteria in the water by boiling the water or bringing the water temperature to 100 degrees centigrade. The same principle applies. If the water boils, its temperature is 100 degrees and, if the water temperature is 100 degrees, the water is boiling. If we truly believe in Jesus, the Holy Spirit comes into our heart automatically and, if we receive the Holy Spirit, it is the result of believing in Jesus.

The Holy Spirit converts the written words of God into living and active words of God (Heb 4:12). The Word of God is the sword of the Spirit (Eph 6:17). It is of no use unless the owner of the sword uses the sword, no matter how good the sword is. No matter how good and powerful the Word of God, it is of no use unless it is applied to life. The Holy Spirit makes the written words of God come alive.

Though Jesus, the Son of God said, "Then you will know the truth, and the truth will set you free" (John 8:32), we are actually set free when the Spirit who is the Spirit of truth, is within us (2 Cor 3:17).

Though Jesus, the Prince of Peace, said, "my peace I give you" (John 14:27), we are at peace when we read or hear the Word because our heart is full of the Holy Spirit. The Holy Spirit fills our heart with peace, which, incidentally, is a fruit of the Spirit.

From the epistles, many words about peace can be found, including, "Grace and peace to you from God our Father and from the Lord Jesus Christ" (Rom 1:7; 1 Cor 1:3; 2 Cor 1:2). But, grace and peace are actually available when the Holy Spirit dwells fully within us.

Dutch theologian Abraham Kuyper said in his book *The Work of the Holy Spirit:*

> He brings every work of the Triune God to its consummation. Hence in the constraining desire of divine love for the individual salvation of chosen but lost creatures, the work of the Holy Spirit evidently occupies the most conspicuous place. So no man can come to the Son but by the Holy Spirit, and no man can know the Son if the Holy Spirit does not reveal Him unto him.[1]

In his thesis, "Paul and the Spirit," Dr. In Kyu Hong said:

> the salvation is beginning by the Holy Spirit and completing by the Holy Spirit, when taking a side view of the experience of the believer.[2]

How important is the role of the Holy Spirit for completing our salvation!

---

1. Kuyper, *The Work of the Holy Spirit*, 211–12.
2. Hong, *Paul and the Holy Spirit*, 446.

9

The Holy Spirit and Sealing

IN THE previous chapter, we learned that being sealed by the Holy Spirit is a deposit that guarantees salvation. Now let us dig deeper into the Bible to see additional truths taught on this critical subject.

> And you also were included in Christ when you heard the word of truth, the gospel of your salvation. Having believed, you were marked in him with a seal, the promised Holy Spirit, who is a deposit guaranteeing our inheritance until the redemption of those who are God's possession—to the praise of his glory. (Eph 1:13–14)

> And do not grieve the Holy Spirit of God, with whom you were sealed for the day of redemption. (Eph 4:30)

> Now it is God who makes both us and you stand firm in Christ. He anointed us, set his seal of ownership on us, and put his Spirit in our hearts as a deposit, guaranteeing what is to come. (2 Cor 1:21–22)

These words from God convincingly teach that those who are definitely saved have "the sealing of the Holy

Spirit," and that they have a secure deposit that guarantees redemption so that they may enter the Kingdom of God.

The definition of "sealing" is "to stamp" something in order to possess it. It is a way of claiming "ownership" or declaring that, "you are mine" (Isa 43:1).

In 2 Corinthians 5:5, we are told, "Now it is God who has made us for this very purpose and has given us the Spirit as a deposit, guaranteeing what is to come."

This means that being "sealed by the Holy Spirit" guarantees salvation because we are positively in God's possession.

We can be sure that being "sealed by the Holy Spirit" guarantees our very salvation!

10

The Holy Spirit and Regeneration

THE MEANING of regeneration in this chapter is "born again with the Holy Spirit." Pastors, theologians, and believers consistently and collectively acknowledge that, based upon biblical teaching, we will—without a doubt—enter the kingdom of heaven when we are born again. Above all things, Jesus Himself said, "no one can enter the Kingdom of God unless he is born again with water and the Holy Spirit" (John 3:3, 5). In other words, salvation is assured through being born again, or through regeneration. On the flip side, without being born again or without regeneration, there is no salvation.

A thorough investigation of Scripture explains why being born again is required in order to enter the Kingdom of God.

Adam and Eve, who were created as God's masterpieces, were deceived by the devil that had taken the shape of a serpent. The crown jewels—mankind—sinned against God by disobeying His commandments (Gen 3:1–19). The words, "for a man is a slave to whatever has mastered him" (2 Pet 2:19) illustrate that all descendants born after Adam and Eve became slaves of the devil—they were born as sinners. According to Romans 6:23, "for the wages of sin is death," all of mankind has fallen into not only physical death, but also spiritual death (hell).

The Holy Spirit and Regeneration 53

In his epistles, the Apostle Paul writes as follows:

> Therefore, just as sin entered the world through one man, and death through sin, and in this way death came to all men, because all sinned. (Rom 5:12)

> As for you, you were dead in your transgressions and sins. (Eph 2:1)

> When you were dead in your sins and in the uncircumcision of your sinful nature . . . . (Col 2:13)

David confessed more seriously in Psalm 51:5:

> Surely I was sinful at birth, sinful from the time my mother conceived me.

Other Scripture verses describing the consequences of man's downfall include:

> The Lord saw how great man's wickedness on the earth had become, and that every inclination of the thoughts of his heart was only evil all the time. (Gen 6:5)

> . . . every inclination of his heart is evil from childhood." (Gen 8:21)

> The hearts of men, moreover, are full of evil. (Eccl 9:3)

> The heart is deceitful above all things and beyond cure. (Jer 17:9)

> For from within, out of men's hearts, come evil thoughts, sexual immorality, theft, murder,

> adultery, greed, malice, deceit, lewdness, envy, slander, arrogance and folly. (Mark 7:21–22)

As a result of these verses, French Reformer John Calvin concluded that this is "total depravity or the natural inability of mankind" as recorded in his book, *Institutes of Christian Religion*. To paraphrase, he continued by saying that the depravity reached into every part of human beings, both body and soul, and that sin spoiled all the abilities of mankind, including the heart and mind. As a result of such natural depravity, mankind is totally incompetent to do any spiritual good. In short, everyone who is not born again is dead.[1]

If this is the case, what is the solution to this problem? Is it possible for human beings to solve it? The answer is "absolutely no!" How can a dead person rise and come to life? No matter how skilled a doctor may be, he cannot revive a dead man. Similarly, human beings do not have enough knowledge or wisdom to correct the original nature of depraved humanity.

No matter how advanced an educational system, or how rich the social, historical, scientific and cultural knowledge may be, none cannot alter mankind. Only the words of God can make a human being born again (1 Pet 1:23). That is, "children born not of natural descent, nor of human decision or a husband's will, but born of God" (John 1:13). The Bible also states that "he saved us, not because of righteous things we had done, but because of his mercy. He saves us through the washing of rebirth and renewal by the Holy Spirit, whom he poured out on us generously through Jesus Christ our Savior" (Titus 3:5–6).

Through Christ, God gives eternal life (Eph 2:5) through the gift of grace (Eph 2:8). Jesus said to Nicodemus, "I tell you the truth, no one can enter the Kingdom of God

1. Steele and Thomas, *The Five Points of Calvinism*, 34–35.

unless he is born of water and the Spirit. Flesh gives birth to flesh, but the Spirit gives birth to spirit" (John 3:5–6). The only way to bring our dead souls—totally depraved and incapable of becoming whole alone—to life is to turn to the Holy Spirit who can make us born again. This is regeneration and the only way to guarantee salvation.

Theologian John Owen says it this way:

> The spring of the whole is the kindness and love of God, even the Father; the procuring cause of the application of that love and kindness to us in Jesus Christ our Savior, in his whole mediation; and the immediate efficient cause in the communication of the Father's love through the Son's mediation, is the Holy Spirit—and this he effects in the renovation of our natures, by the washing of regeneration, wherein we are purged from our sins, and sanctified to God. This great truth, that the Holy Spirit is the author of our regeneration (which the ancients esteemed a cogent argument to prove his deity, from the greatness and dignity of the work) is, in words, at least, generally granted by all who pretend to sobriety in Christianity.[2]

Keep in mind that "regeneration" and "sealing with the Holy Spirit" are one and the same; they serve as a deposit guaranteeing salvation.

Further investigation of regeneration illustrates that it is connected to the sealing of the Holy Spirit and, especially, to the baptism with the Holy Spirit. I will explain more details about the baptism of the Holy Spirit in the next chapter. But it is important to touch on the relationship between regeneration and baptism with the Holy Spirit because this is crucial for the work of salvation.

2. Owen, *The Holy Spirit*, 149.

Many theologians insist that both regeneration and baptism of the Holy Spirit guarantee salvation and occur at the same time. However, although some theologians agree that both regeneration and baptism of the Holy Spirit guarantee salvation, but insist that they happen at different times. Still other theologians, specifically those of the Pentecostal faith, agree that regeneration guarantees salvation, but they are resolute that baptism of the Holy Spirit is not related to salvation and that it is a "second blessing" available to saints who are born again.

As I believe both regeneration and baptism with the Holy Spirit guarantee salvation and happen at the same time, I would like to present evidence that supports this point of view:

A. Those who believe that both regeneration and baptism of the Holy Spirit guarantee salvation but happened at different times.

B. Those who believe that baptism of the Holy Spirit is not related to salvation and is a second blessing.

In order to avoid any complication, "baptism with the Holy Spirit" means that this baptism happened at Pentecost.

The insistence of theologians who ascribe to summary statement *A,* that the disciples of Jesus Christ were already born again before Pentecost, can be disputed on the basis of several scriptural passages. Specifically, it is impossible to say that Peter, who confessed, "You are the Christ, the Son of the living God" (Matt 16:16), was not born again. If regeneration and baptism of the Holy Spirit are both salvation, as believed by these same theologians, then it appears the disciples received salvation twice. Must we be saved two times? Of course not! It is enough to be saved one time!

Some Pentecostal theologians who believe as summarized in statement *B* hold the same opinion as statement *A,* that the disciples of Jesus Christ were already born again

The Holy Spirit and Regeneration 57

before Pentecost, except they regard the Pentecost as a second blessing. Detailed explanations of this discrepancy are presented in chapter 11, *The Holy Spirit and Baptism*. Evidence that statement *B* does not correspond with the Bible is disclosed in that chapter.

Taking an in-depth look at the time of regeneration, the following words of the Bible offer a biblical framework for theologians who insist that the disciples were born again before Pentecost.

First, "no one who is speaking by the Spirit of God says, 'Jesus be cursed,' and no one can say, 'Jesus is Lord,' except by the Holy Spirit" (1 Cor 12:3).

Second, "Simon Peter answered, 'You are the Christ, the Son of the living God'" (Matt 16:16).

Third, "Jesus answered, 'A person who has had a bath needs only to wash his feet; his whole body is clean, though not every one of you'" (John 13:10).

Fourth, "You are already clean because of the word I have spoken to you" (John 15:3).

As for the first statement, we have repeatedly discovered in this chapter that "the Holy Spirit and salvation," to reiterate, those who are born again with the Holy Spirit, have absolutely confessed "Jesus as Lord." Even though they confess "Jesus as Lord," not all of them are born again with the Holy Spirit. They can confess "Jesus as Lord" as many times as they wish and even then are not necessarily born again with the Holy Spirit. That is the reason why Jesus, the Son of God, said in Matthew 7:21, "Not everyone who says to me, 'Lord, Lord,' will enter the kingdom of heaven." Doesn't this mean that those who cannot enter the kingdom of heaven are not born again with the Holy Spirit?

As for the second statement, the reason Peter confessed, "you are Christ and Son of the living God" (Matt 16:16), is not because he was born again with the Holy Spirit, but rather, God the Father in heaven provided this opportunity for Peter to acknowledge that He (God) moved through the Holy Spirit. If Peter was born again at that time, how could he have acted as a perpetrator of the devil? Remember, he denied Jesus three times, called down curses on him, deserted and, ultimately, fled from Jesus (Matt 16:23; 26:33–34, 56; 74–75). He, of course, did not curse Jesus, but himself. Suppose he was born again with the Holy Spirit. If so, his hope lies in the kingdom of heaven and he need not have strayed far.

As for third statement, Scripture clearly shows that the disciples were born again based on Jesus' words, "you are clean." If this is the case, when did the disciples become clean? By what words of Jesus did they become clean? If the disciples were clean as a result of Jesus' words, why was Iscariot Judas unclean? Remember, he betrayed Jesus after taking part in the Last Supper (Matt 26:18–28). It is understood that no one was clean until that time. Let us examine this further.

In the Bible, many prophecies are written in the past or present perfect tense since some of these prophecies are yet to be realized, but certainly shall be fulfilled in the future. For example, in Isaiah 40:2, the prophecy regarding the Messiah was written in present perfect tense:

> Speak tenderly to Jerusalem, and proclaim to her that her hard service has been completed, that *her sin has been paid for*, that she has received from the Lord's hand double to all her sins.

The above words of prophecy relate to the birth of Jesus, the Messiah, which was to occur in the future, approximately 750 years later. Because the prophecy of the birth of Jesus was so obvious, the Bible used the present perfect tense—*her sin has been paid for*—instead of future tense, in spite of the fact that it would not take place until some 750 years later.

In John 16:33, Jesus said, "In this world you will have trouble. But take heart! *I have overcome* the world." In this phrase, "the world" means "the prince of this world" (John 16:11) who is the devil holding the power of death (Heb 2:14). The time that the Lord Jesus has actually overcome the power of death is after He dies and is resurrected. In spite of the above fact, the Bible uses the present perfect tense—*I have overcome*—because the prophecy is so obvious.

If Peter and all of the other disciples were already born again before Pentecost, they could not desert their Lord and run away in fear for their lives, because they would already have received a guarantee that they would enter the kingdom of heaven after death. As Jesus knew definitely that His disciples would be born again when the Holy Spirit came, He used the present perfect tense, "You are already clean because of the word I have spoken to you." (John 15:3). We can become clean only when the Holy Spirit, the Spirit of Holiness—symbolized as water, fire, and wind—comes into our heart.

Some theologians are adamant that the disciples were born again when Jesus breathed on them and said, "Receive the Holy Spirit" (John 20:22)! But this is also not correct. Jesus' action is a form of "behavior prophecy," given to illustrate that He, who is the last Adam and a life-giving spirit, gives the disciples a great commission. They are commissioned to boldly witness to the ends of the earth after receiving the power of the Holy Spirit, the One who breathed into the nostril of Adam—the first man—in order to transform and give him life. A prophet named Agabus used similar behavior prophecy in Acts 21:10–14. He prophesied—through his behavior—of what would happen in the future.

If the disciples received the Holy Spirit when Jesus said, "Receive the Holy Spirit!" there is no explanation as to why they did not go out immediately to preach the Gospel but, rather, went out to fish the same as they had before meeting with Jesus. If they received the Holy Spirit at that time, the words of Jesus: "Do not leave Jerusalem, but wait for the gift my Father promised, which you have heard me speak about. For John baptized with water, but in a few days you will be baptized with the Holy Spirit" (Acts 1:4–5), would also be incorrect.

Regeneration represents "born again with the Holy Spirit" and "up to that time, the Spirit had not been given" (John 7:39b). It is illogical to believe, then, that the disciples were born again of the Holy Spirit, the Spirit of truth who came upon them at Pentecost for the first time.

Consequently, regeneration, which means to be "born again of the Holy Spirit," occurred when they received the Holy Spirit on Pentecost for the first time. In other words, regeneration is baptism of the Holy Spirit and baptism of the Holy Spirit is regeneration. Each is the same event that happened simultaneously and is merely looked at from different points of view.

11

The Holy Spirit and Baptism

FOR THE sake of clarification, I would like to state upfront that "baptism" with the Holy Spirit means the same as "baptized" with the Holy Spirit. This point is important to note because the noun "baptism" is not written in the Bible. In this chapter we will use biblical evidence to dispute the insistence of a portion of the Pentecostal community's claim that "baptism with the Holy Spirit" has nothing to do with salvation, but rather, is a second blessing given to born again saints. Biblical evidence will show that this theory is incorrect.

The first error in the Pentecostal school of thought is in looking only at the outward works of the Holy Spirit at Pentecost, as written in Acts 2. Practitioners focus on the words, "filled with the Holy Spirit" and on "tongues." Speaking in tongues is a gift of the Holy Spirit. It is true, those filled with the Holy Spirit in biblical times spoke in other tongues. But, it is important to understand the intention of the Holy Spirit and for what purpose He let them be filled with the Holy Spirit in order to speak other tongues.

Speaking in tongues is one of the nine spiritual gifts of the Holy Spirit (1 Cor 12:4–10) and one of the signs accompanying those who believe (Mark 16:17). Actually, speaking in tongues is not related to salvation even though, in the book of Acts, it is clear that those who spoke in tongues were baptized with the Holy Spirit (Acts 10:45–46, 19:6). In the era of the Old Testament, all of the gifts of the Holy Spirit were given except tongues and the ability to interpret of tongues. These gifts appeared at Pentecost for the first time.

For what profound reasons might God have given such gifts? It is my contention that the Lord, who confused the language in earlier days, wanted to unify His people into one spiritual language in these last days. He did this as a tangible sign that the new era had come. When focusing on the event of Pentecost itself, I believe the gift of tongues was given for the express purpose of drawing in crowds and then performing works of salvation such as preaching the Gospel. Pentecostal theologians overlook God's intention, which was to show people that salvation is an inward transformation. He wanted to illustrate that the inward works of the Holy Spirit bring outward manifestations such as "tongues" (Acts 2:1–4, 10:44–46, 19:6).

The second error of Pentecostal thinking is in looking at Pentecost as a simple event when, in fact, it was an event the Father and the Son had promised for many years. The event of Pentecost was forecast many times as Jesus told His disciples:

> I am going to send you what my Father has promised; but stay in the city until you have been clothed with power from on high. (Luke 24:49)

> On one occasion, while he was eating with them, he gave them this command: 'Do not leave Jerusalem, but wait for the gift my Father promised, which you have heard me speak about. For John baptized with water, but in a few days you will be baptized with the Holy Spirit.' (Acts 1:4–5)

> But you will receive power when the Holy Spirit comes on you; and you will be my witnesses in Jerusalem, and in all Judea and Samaria, and to the ends of the earth. (Acts 1:8)

This is also testified through the mouth of the Apostle Peter:

> Exalted to the right hand of God, he has received from the Father the promised Holy Spirit and has poured out what you now see and hear. (Acts 2:33)

We have to pay attention to the fact that the event of Pentecost means "baptized with the Holy Spirit" as Jesus said to His disciples, and this baptizing with the Holy Spirit was accomplished according to the words that the Father had already promised. The Apostle Peter quoted one phrase of this promise when he said:

> In the last days, God says,
> I will pour out my Spirit on all people.
> Your sons and daughters will prophesy,
> your young men will see visions,
> your old men will dream dreams.
> Even on my servants, both men and women,
> I will pour out my Spirit in those days,
> And they will prophecy.
> I will show wonders in the heaven above
> And signs on the earth below,
> blood and fire and billows of smoke.
> The sun will be turned to darkness
> and the moon to blood
> before the coming of the great and glorious
> day of the Lord.
> And everyone who calls
> on the name of the Lord will be saved.
> (Acts 2:17–21)

The Apostle Peter explained that the words of the Prophet Joel had been fulfilled (Joel 2:28–32).

Prophecies regarding the Holy Spirit promised by the Father are written not only in Joel but also by other prophets in the Old Testament. Although there are many prophecies, I have chosen to review the following two samples:

> till the Spirit is poured upon us from on high,
> and the desert becomes a fertile field,
> and the fertile field seems like a forest.
> Justice will dwell in the desert
> and righteousness live in the fertile field.
> The fruit of the righteousness will be peace;
> the effect of righteousness will be quietness
> and confidence forever. (Isa 32:15–17)

> And I will put my Spirit in you and move you to follow my decrees and be careful to keep my laws. You will live in the land I gave your forefathers; you will be my people, and I will be your God. (Ezek 36:27–28)

Many of the words promised in the Old Testament have to do with the *relationship* between the people and God or God and the people. The fact is that in the future, God will give a new and better covenant that is the *true relationship* between God and the people. This is only possible through the Counselor, the Spirit, who is the Spirit of the Lord and the Spirit of God. Jesus, the Son of God, commanded His disciples not to leave Jerusalem until the Spirit comes. He wanted the disciples to wait for the Holy Spirit to come upon them, and for them to serve as witnesses.

The third error of the Pentecostal school of thought is that it discounts the purpose of baptism of the Holy Spirit—a purpose that is repeatedly promised in relation to providing salvation—not given as one of the gifts. A few conservative theologians insist that "baptized with the Holy Spirit" as spoken of in 1 Corinthians 12:13 is the same as salvation, while "the baptism of the Holy Spirit" at Pentecost was given for a different reason—to distribute various spiritual gifts. If this is so, I question why God repeatedly promised baptism of the Holy Spirit at Pentecost? I would ask Pentecostal believers why they make different distinctions about the baptism of the Holy Spirit when God uses the same words in Scripture?

The Bible testifies to the many miracles, wonders, and signs experienced by numerous prophets and servants of the Lord during Old and New Testament times. The disciples of Jesus had carried out lots of miracles and wonders, and driven out many demons (Matt 10:1, 8; Mark 6:7, 13; Luke 9:1, 10:17–19). Peter is the only person to ever walk on water in the history of the power of the Holy Spirit (Matt 14:29)! However, it makes sense to understand the intention of the Lord. As related to the baptism of the Spirit, it is important to ascertain why the disciples chose not to leave Jerusalem though they had obviously been given power. Not even at that time, not even in Jerusalem, could God give them unlimited power! That was yet to come.

Pentecost is a key eschatological event because, throughout the world, it serves as a witness to the power of the Holy Spirit and a dramatic event demonstrating the purpose of Pentecost as the salvation of souls.

Actually, the event that must precede Pentecost is the virgin birth of the Son of God. This is so because *the promised Holy Spirit* cannot come unless the Son of God who is without sin comes to this world in the flesh, sheds His blood on the cross, dies, is resurrected, and goes up to heaven (John 16:7). God the Father promised the "Messiah" (Christ) and a new Spirit and he always fulfills His promises.

If we are to summarize the Old Testament in just a few words, it has to be "Messiah will come" and the New Testament summary is "Messiah has come and will come again." God the Father had no other way but to send His one and only Son in order to save His chosen people in the world. He allowed His Son to be born of the Virgin Mary and said, through His angel, "She will give birth to a son, and you are to give him the name Jesus, because he will save his people from their sins" (Matt 1:21). From this verse, we can determine, with absolute certainty, God the Father's reason for giving the name "Jesus" to His Son. Through Jesus, He is "to save his people from their sins." The most important and great purpose of Jesus is *salvation*!

Now let us explore how Jesus became the Savior.

John the Baptist appears in the Gospels of the New Testament and is probably best known for baptizing people in water to prepare the way for the Lord. In truth, he is born into this world by the power of the Holy Spirit in order to testify about Jesus, and is later killed by King Herod (Matt 14:1–12; Mark 6:14–29). His essential mission is *to testify that Jesus is the Messiah*. The first testimony to which John the Baptist bears witness is in signifying that Jesus is "the Lamb of God, who takes away the sin of the world" (John 1:29). This means that Jesus will die and shed blood for the redemption of all our sins.

There are many references in the Bible affirming that all people in this world are born sinners:

> There is no one righteous, not even one. (Rom 3:10)

> There is no difference, for all have sinned and fall short of the glory of God. (Rom 3:23)

Therefore, everyone in this world will die, not only physically but spiritually, because the law of "the wages of sin is death" (Rom 6:23). Without the promise of Jesus' redemption, everyone would go to hell.

According to the words "without the shedding of blood there is no forgiveness" (Heb 9:22), it is apparent that someone must shed blood for the redemption of sins. Because "it is impossible for the blood of bulls and goats to take away sins" (Heb 10:4) and only the blood of Jesus is without sin (Heb 4:15; 1 Pet 2:22; 1 John 3:5), He alone can purify us from all sins (Heb 9:12; 1 John 1:7). Jesus is the only one to qualify as "the Lamb of God who takes away the sin of the world." Therefore, Jesus was called the "Passover Lamb" whose blood made it possible for the Israelites to be freed from slavery in Egypt (Exod 12:1–12; 1 Cor 5:7).

There is a problem, however. It is impossible to complete the work of salvation *only* by shedding the blood of Jesus. While suffering in agony on the cross, Jesus prayed to the Father, asking Him to forgive all the sins of the world.(Luke 23:34). As such, everyone in the world should have been forgiven their sins and given eternal life. But that is not the case. John the Baptist, who served a key role, testified about Jesus saying, "He will baptize with the Holy Spirit" (Matt 3:11; Mark 1:8; Luke 3:16; John 1:33).

Why do you think John the Baptist testified as above? It is because the Son of God is a Savior, first by offering Himself as a sacrifice for the forgiveness of our sins and second, by baptizing with the Holy Spirit.

The above words are written in all four Gospels. Obviously there is great significance when a message is written in all four Gospels. Here is a sampling of these words:

- He will baptize you with the Holy Spirit and with fire (Matt 3:11)
- He will baptize you with the Holy Spirit (Mark 1:8)
- He will baptize you with the Holy Spirit and with fire (Luke 3:16)

- He who will baptize with the Holy Spirit (John 1:33)

The verses are all written in the future tense. The same words are also written in Acts as "you will be baptized with the Holy Spirit" (Acts 1:5, 11:16), but they are delivered in the passive future tense because Jesus said them personally. 1 Corinthians 12:13 says that "we were all baptized by one Spirit into one body." Please note that this verse is written in passive past tense because the people had already become one body after being baptized by the Holy Spirit.

Jesus, the Son of God, commanded His disciples not to leave Jerusalem and to wait for this gift in order to keep His promise of *the baptism with the Holy Spirit* as testified by John the Baptist. In addition, Jesus indirectly told to His disciples several other things regarding the baptism of the Holy Spirit.

> I tell you the truth, some who are standing here will not taste death before they see the Son of Man coming in his Kingdom. (Matt 16:28)

Here, the Son of Man means Counselor, the Holy Spirit, with the name of Jesus, who is also the Spirit of the Sovereign Lord (Isa 61:1), who rules as a King of His Kingdom.

> And surely I am with you always, to the very end of the age. (Matt 28:20)

This word confirms what Jesus said in John 14:16–23. That is, Jesus will be with us forever in the form of Counselor, who is the Spirit of truth as well as the Spirit of Jesus.

> Whoever believes and is baptized will be saved. (Mark 16:16)

A second Scripture reference in the book of John means to be "born again with water and the Holy Spirit"

(John 3:3-5), which can easily be interpreted as "baptism with the Holy Spirit."

Among the many descriptors used to express "the Holy Spirit," the word "Counselor" must be considered carefully. On the last and greatest day of the feast, Jesus stood and said in a loud voice:

> 'If anyone is thirsty, let him come to me and drink. Whoever believes in me, as the Scripture has said, streams of living water will flow from within him.' By this he meant the Spirit, whom those who believed in him were late to receive. Up to that time the Spirit had not been given, since Jesus had not yet been glorified. (John 7:37–39)

Jesus said that when another Counselor who is the Spirit of the truth comes, he will be with us forever (John 14:16–17). Jesus Himself is Counselor—*Parakleto* in Greek (1 John 2:1)—and promised to send another Counselor. In English, the word "another" is defined as "additional one of the same kind or very similar qualities but with different shape or form."

The reason Jesus said "another Counselor" is that "the Holy Spirit as Counselor" has the same substance and character of Jesus, though a different image from "Counselor as Spirit." In the words of Jesus:

> But I tell you the truth: It is for your good that I am going away. Unless I go away, the Counselor will not come to you; but if I go, I will send him to you. (John 16:7)

Here, He is telling the disciples that He can send the Counselor only after He dies, is raised from the dead, taken up to heaven, sits sat at the right hand of the throne of God, and is glorified. The explanation is stated more directly in John 7:39:

> By this he meant the Spirit, whom those believed in him were later to receive. Up to that time the Spirit had not been given, since Jesus had not yet been glorified.

Therefore, the Apostle Peter said, "Exalted to the right hand of God, he has received from the Father the promised Holy Spirit and has poured out what you now see and hear" (Acts 2:33), and also Jesus said before going away to heaven, "but in a few days, you would be baptized with the Holy Spirit" (Acts 1:5).

Pentecost was a wonderful event in which the Counselor, the Holy Spirit, came to this world for the first time and entered into God's chosen people as *the living water*. This event confirmed the testimony of John the Baptist that He (Jesus) would become our savior by "baptizing with the Holy Spirit."

In conjunction with Pentecost, the words "my name" may even hold more prominence than that of "Counselor." John 14:26 reads:

> but the Counselor, the Holy Spirit, whom the Father will send in *my name* will teach you all things and will remind you of everything I have said to you.

In other words, the Counselor, the Holy Spirit, will come in "my name" which is "the name of the Son of God" or "Jesus." Salvation can be completed only when the Counselor, the Holy Spirit with Jesus' name, comes into us.

Before moving on, let us summarize the relationship between Jesus, the Son of God, and the baptism with the Holy Spirit. The reason Jesus, the Son of God, is our savior is that He shed His blood, rose from the dead, was taken up to heaven, gave "the name Jesus" to the Holy Spirit, and poured out "the Holy Spirit as Counselor" (baptizing with the Holy Spirit). First he did this for the 120 disciples and later to all people who believed in Jesus, effectively creating what is known as the body of Christ.

These are the last words Jesus said to His disciples before going to heaven:

> But you will receive power when the Holy Spirit comes on you; and you will be my witnesses in Jerusalem, and in all Judea and Samaria, and to the ends of the earth. (Acts 1:8)

Pentecostal followers error in believing that the word "power" associates only with "spiritual gifts" appearing outwardly. Actually, at this point Jesus has already given authority and power to His disciples. Understanding the intention of the Lord Jesus in this situation, that He commanded His disciples not to leave Jerusalem until they received the Holy Spirit and His power, discredits the Pentecostal position.

How would you define the *power of powers* and *miracle of miracles?* Certainly they would not be considered the ultimate sacrifice if one sinner simply repented, was saved, and went to heaven after death. Jesus expounds upon His power by saying:

> What good will it be for a man if he gains the whole world, yet forfeits his soul? Or what can a man give in exchange for his soul? (Matt 16:26)

One soul is extremely valuable when it can be exchanged for the whole world! Suppose you are so powerful that you can create or eliminate the whole world with a single word. Yet, this power is of no use if your soul goes to hell. The power capable of saving souls must have *Jesus' name*, and those who are saved must have *the name of*

Jesus. Once the name of Jesus is within, the Gospel can be preached boldly. Though all of the disciples have received power from Jesus and have driven out demons, they all ran away on the night Jesus was arrested because they had yet to receive *the name of Jesus* at that time.

The disciples truly believed in Jesus. (John 2:11, 22–23).It was by no means a lie to pledge not to disown Jesus even if they had to die with Him (Matt 26:35; Luke 22:33; John 13:37), but they still ran away when their lives were in danger. Even though they had talked with Jesus after His resurrection, they were instructed to return to their lives as fishermen until they could receive *the name of Jesus* within their hearts.

Though the Son of God was fully aware of this situation, He could not give the name "Jesus" during His lifetime—only after He died, rose, and went to heaven through the Counselor, the Spirit. After that, the disciples could become true witnesses.

Remember, the Lord Jesus did not say, "be my witnesses" but "will be my witnesses" (Acts 1:8). To be witnesses is not by His commandment but occurs automatically only after receipt of the Counselor, the Holy Spirit. The most important role among the works of the Counselor is to testify about Jesus (John 15:26), because He has the *name of Jesus.* Because *the name Jesus* has absolute authority (Eph 1:21; Phil 2:9–10), believers can testify about Jesus—preach the Gospel—even to the point of death. The Greek word for "witness" is "*martus,*" which translates to "martyr" in English. Thereafter, most of the disciples, apostles, and apostolic fathers died as martyrs for the Gospel, confirming the words of God:

> When the Counselor comes, whom I will send to you from the Father, the Spirit of truth who goes out from the Father, he will testify about

The Holy Spirit and Baptism

me. And you also must testify, for you have been with me from the beginning. (John 15:26–27)

We are witnesses of these things, and so is the Holy Spirit, whom God has given to those who obey him. (Acts 5:32)

The Spirit and the bride say, 'Come!' And let him who hears say, 'Come!' Whoever is thirsty, let him come; and whoever wishes, let him take the free gift of the water of life. (Rev 22:17)

The above words demonstrate that when the Counselor comes, we—the church as His bride—preach the Gospel together with the Counselor, the Holy Spirit. The Holy Spirit testifies to Jesus only and Jesus wants to be testified only by the Holy Spirit. Therefore, the easiest way to determine whether someone is baptized with the Holy Spirit is to observe whether he preaches the Gospel.

When the Counselor, the Holy Spirit, comes, manifestations of the Holy Spirit are normally apparent. After Pentecost, the powers of the Holy Spirit were evidenced continuously through the disciples. They did not use their new spiritual gifts for personal gain, but used them to preach the Gospel and invite others to accept "the name of Jesus" in order to gain salvation. The disciples—who ran away previously in fear of their lives—now, being baptized with the Holy Spirit, preached the Gospel of Jesus Christ without holding their lives dear.

Why is the name of Jesus so important? The Bible reveals details into the power behind Jesus' name:

- The crippled man is walking in the name of Jesus (Acts 3:6–7)
- miraculous signs and wonders through the name of Jesus (Acts 4:30)

- when preaching the Gospel in the name of Jesus, lots of people were saved (Acts 2:41, 4:4)
- Jesus is the only name by which we are saved. (Acts 4:12)
- everyone who calls on the name of the Lord (Jesus) will be saved. (Acts 2:21; Rom 10:13; Joel 2:32; Ps 116:4)
- at the name of Jesus, every knee should bow, in heaven and on earth and under the earth. (Phil 2:10)

The name "Jesus" yields enormous power and, as such, the devil hates and fears His name. Satan threatened the disciples, forbidding them to speak or teach in the name of Jesus, (Acts 4:17–18; 5:40, and persecuted them when they used His name (Acts 5:41; 1 Pet 4:14). To this day, the devil works tirelessly and craftily to prevent believers from drawing power from Jesus' name and spreading its power. By seducing believers where we are personally weak, Satan causes us to fall into sin that serves to diminish our faith. Christians who have fallen in faith do not preach the Gospel strongly and courageously, nor do they display powerful abilities in the name of Jesus. This is a critical issue and one I will discuss more fully in chapter 18, *The Name of the Holy Spirit.*

To date we have learned three ways in which the Holy Spirit works:

1. Sealing with the Holy Spirit
2. Born again with the Holy Spirit (regeneration)
3. Baptized with the Holy Spirit (baptism with the Holy Spirit)

Each of these phrases represents salvation. When a person is baptized with the Holy Spirit, he or she is born again and sealed with the Holy Spirit all at the same time.

It is also important to understand biblical references to the following phrases and words: "received the Holy Spirit from the Father," "has poured out the Holy Spirit," "I will send the Holy Spirit," "receive," "pour," and "send." We do not want to mistakenly conclude that the Holy Spirit is inferior to the Father or the Son. As illustrated previously, the Father, Son, and Holy Spirit are perfect, identical persons in every respect. The Holy Spirit has come in the name of Jesus and is linked directly to salvation. When the Holy Spirit comes into God's chosen people, words such as "received" are used in the Bible. In other words, the Holy Spirit comes only into the people the Father chose before the creation of the world (Eph 1:4), the people given to his Son Jesus (John 6:37–40, 65) and the people who truly believed in Jesus.

Pentecost might not be repeated again but baptism with the Holy Spirit is taking place frequently all over the world to this day.

For those who would like to be baptized with the Holy Spirit, three methods are demonstrated in the Bible:

1. Join together constantly in prayer in one place (Acts 1:14, 2:1)
2. Place hands on those who want to be baptized with the Holy Spirit (Acts 8:17, 9:17, 19:6)
3. Listen to the words of God (Acts 10:44)

In addition to the above examples, the Apostle Peter said:

> Repent and be baptized, every one of you, in the name of Jesus Christ for the forgiveness of your sins. And you will receive the gift of the Holy Spirit. (Acts 2:38)

And lastly, Jesus commanded:

> Find, seek and knock, and then the Father in heaven will give the Holy Spirit. (Luke 11:9–13)

Judging from the above examples, there is no other way to be baptized with the Holy Spirit, but through the

Word and prayer. All the examples except one are the result of prayer. The best way to be baptized with the Holy Spirit is prayer! The wonderful works of the Holy Spirit will surely be with you all when you meet together and pray together!

12

The Holy Spirit and the Church

JESUS, THE Son of God, came to this world to fulfill a primary purpose: "to seek and to save what was lost" (Luke 19:10), "to expect for the sons of God to be revealed" (Rom 8:19), "to destroy the devil's work" (1 John 3:8), and that His name might be proclaimed over all the earth through the children of God who are saved (Acts 9:15; Rom 9:17; Exod 9:16; Deut 32:3). In a word—salvation—is why Jesus came and He expects it to be accomplished through the church. "On this rock, I will build my church," Jesus said (Matt 16:18). The rock is Jesus Himself, the name of Jesus, and the confession of the saints proclaiming, "You are the Christ and Son of the living God" (Matt 16:16).

As we can see, "I will build my church" is written in the future tense. At the time the church was actually built, the Counselor, the Holy Spirit, appeared for the first time at Pentecost. Someone might cite "the assembly in the desert" (Acts 7:38) as proof that a church existed in the era of the Old Testament. But that is not the church (*ekklesia* in Greek) founded by our Lord Jesus. In this chapter we will discuss, strictly from a church doctrinal viewpoint, the relationship between the Holy Spirit and the church.

There are several names and symbols of the New Testament church that theologians say represent other images of the church. Names include, "people of God," "body of Jesus Christ," and "temple of the Holy Spirit." In this chapter, however, I would like to define the church using three different images. I have chosen to examine "children of God" instead of "people of God," which will be addressed separately. Today, we will discuss:

A. Children of God (John 1:12, 11:52; Gal 3:26)
B. Body of Jesus Christ (Eph 1:22–23; Col 1:18, 24)
C. Temple of the Holy Spirit (1 Cor 3:16, 6:19)

Please note that in the Bible, the church is expressed many times as the "church of God" or "God's church" (1 Cor 1:2, 10:32, 11:16, 22; 2 Cor 1:1; 2 Thess 1:4; 1 Tim 3:5). God's church is interpreted as "church of the Father," "church of the Son," and "church of the Holy Spirit" to reflect the Trinity of God.

Now, let us examine the relationship between the Trinity of God and the three different images of the church.

In looking at the first image, "children of God," the Apostle John writes: "Yet to all who received him, to those who believed in his name, he gave the right to become children of God" (John 1:12). The most important right among the rights of children of God is that they are able to enter the Kingdom of God. This is salvation. The word "children" is used in relation to a parent or father, as it reinforces the concept of "God the Father" caring for His "children of God."

On what grounds do the father and son call each other "father" and "son"? Certainly the son cannot testify or give evidences that the father is truly his father. No one bears witness to his actual birth. A father recognizes his child and presents him to the world by saying, "this is my son." In the Bible, God says, "You are my Son; today I have become your Father" (Heb 1:5, 5:5; Ps 2:7).

How can God the Father make us His children? He officially sealed us with the Holy Spirit and said, "You are my son, today I have become your Father" (Romans 8:14–16). Just as the owner of a ranch brands his initial(s) onto the buttocks of his cattle with a mark that will never vanish, our Father in heaven also seals us with the Holy Spirit and makes us His eternal children.

In West Africa, whenever I speak of the above parable to pastors attending the pneumatology seminar—many of who are black—they understand quickly. As you know, many of them still bear the scars of war on their faces.

One day I asked: "Dear pastor, what do the scars on your face mean?"

He replied: "This means we are from the same family."

Today there are still lots of different tribes living in West Africa and each tribe bears a different facial scar. Their customs and languages are different; they cannot communicate with each other. There are approximately seventy tribes in Burkina Faso where I speak. Even in this twenty-first century, the tribes are at war with each other, but not nearly as much as in the past! It was probably very difficult to distinguish who was who, especially at night, because the color of their skin is also dark. By making a scar on the face, the most visible part of the body, soldiers could decipher their own tribesmen. This concept of ownership, knowing who you belong to, or being told "you are family" is similarly practiced by God.

In the Bible, the Spirit, the Spirit of sonship, testifies to our spirit that we are God's children, and to Him we cry out to God, our Abba Father (Rom 8:15–16). We can call upon our "Abba Father" only after the Spirit who is the Spirit of his Son comes into our heart (Gal 4:6). Once we become children of God, by having the Holy Spirit in our heart, we are His forever (John 14:16).

God the Father makes us His children *by sealing us with the Holy Spirit*. It is of no use to say, "Our father in heaven" in our prayers unless we have the Counselor, the Holy Spirit, in our heart.

The second image of the church that we will explore is "the body of Jesus Christ." The concept of "body" is connected to Jesus, the Son of God, who came into this world with a physical body. For this reason, He called the church "His body." If we are counted among the body of Jesus Christ, we can, of course, enter the Kingdom of God. We have salvation.

In truth though, how can Jesus, the Son of God, make us His body? He does so by baptizing with the Holy Spirit. We can be a part of the "body of Jesus Christ" only when we are baptized with the Holy Spirit who is also "the Spirit of Jesus Christ." The Apostle Paul described this fact clearly in 1 Corinthians 12:13:

"For we were all baptized by one Spirit into one body—whether Jews or Greeks, slave or free—and we were all given the one Spirit to drink."

The only way to unite us into one body is to be baptized with the Holy Spirit. Jesus, the Son of God became our savior by baptizing us with the Holy Spirit through which we become part of the body of Jesus Christ.

In an examination of the third image of the church, "the temple of the Holy Spirit," we find the house or temple where the Holy Spirit dwells. When the Holy Spirit is within us, we become the "temple of the Holy Spirit," that is "holy house," The Catholic or Orthodox Church designates the title of "saint" to an extraordinary person. However, saint within this context describes a person who has received the Holy Spirit and, as such, joins with others who have also received the Holy Spirit. This company of believers is called "saints" and is written about many times in the Bible. The name "saints" distinguishes Christians from other people in the world. Therefore, all who are born again with the Holy Spirit are saints and individually, each is a "saint."

The Son of God called Himself a "temple" (John 2:19–21), while Jesus referred to Himself as the "Holy One of God" (Mark 1:24; Luke 4:34). When the Holy Spirit, who is also the Spirit of Holiness, dwells within us, we become the "Temple of the Holy Spirit."

Now, how can the Holy Spirit make us "the temple of the Holy Spirit?" By becoming "born again with the Holy Spirit," The Holy Spirit transforms believers into the "temple of the Holy Spirit" through regeneration.

I have explained how the Trinity of God transforms us into "the church of God" as illustrated in the following simple chart:

Trinity of God	Method of Salvation	Image of Church
Father	Sealing with the Spirit	Children of God
Son	Baptizing with the Spirit	Body of Christ
Spirit	Born again with the Spirit	Temple of the Spirit

Each of these actions uses a different method to help believers secure salvation and become a part of the church, according to the works of the Trinity of God. A key factor yet to be stated, is that God the Father cannot make us His children without the Holy Spirit (sealing with the Holy Spirit) and the Son of God cannot make us His Body without the Holy Spirit (baptism with the Holy Spirit). Each person of the Trinity of God carries equal authority in granting salvation, but the Holy Spirit bears an even more important role among them. A full explanation of the roles of the Father, the Son, and the Holy Spirit are explored in chapters 4, 5, and 8.

Now let us explore the relationship between "God and the people."

In Genesis 17:10–14, God, the Lord, established an everlasting covenant with Abraham that required all male Israelites and foreigners in their households to be circumcised in order to become "the people of God." Those who refused would be cut off from His people. Even the Israelites would be cut off from God's people unless they circumcised their flesh. After entering into the covenant, God said, "circumcise your hearts" (Deut 10:16) and "I will circumcise your heart" (Deut 30:6).

We know that the above words were achieved in the New Testament. The Apostle Paul said in Romans 2:28–29:

> A man is not a Jew if he is only one outwardly, nor is circumcision merely outward and physical. No, a man is a Jew if he is one inwardly; and circumcision is circumcision of the heart by the Spirit, not by the written code. Such a man's praise is not from men, but from God.

Paul explained that true Jews should have circumcision of the heart by the Spirit, not circumcision of the flesh by the written code. If they resist the Holy Spirit, they are unable to be circumcised in their hearts (Acts 7:51).

In the relationship between "God and the people," which is the other image of the church, people are disqualified as "God's people" in cases where there is no spiritual circumcision of the heart. In finality, there is no salvation. To clarify, the Holy Spirit transforms "saints" or "God's people" and makes them "overseers of the church of God" (Acts 20:28).

I would like to emphasize that "baptism with the Holy Spirit" is when "the Counselor, the Holy Spirit with the name of Jesus" comes into our hearts. Through this action, we are "born again with the Holy Spirit" (regeneration) and "sealed with the Holy Spirit." This happens simultaneously and is the only way to become a member of the true church of God—the only way to salvation!

13

The Double Works of the Holy Spirit

To date, various works of the Holy Spirit have been reviewed. As a matter of fact, a saint (one who is born again) can do *nothing* in his family or social life inside or outside of the church, and nothing can happen in the world or universe, without intervention by the Holy Spirit. As discussed previously, all works written about in the Bible were actually carried out by the Holy Spirit.

It is interesting to note that although most of the works of the Holy Spirit are related to the salvation of the souls, others are not directly related. Actions such as healing or driving out the demons fall into the latter category. I refer to these works as "the double works of the Holy Spirit." Although other theologians have commented on this subject, I will address matters that have remained unclear. The foundation of this discussion is based upon John 7:39:

> By this he meant the Spirit, whom those who believed in him were later to receive. Up to that time the Spirit had not been given, since Jesus had not yet been glorified.

In the previous passage, Jesus said, "Whoever believes in me, as the Scripture has said, streams of living water will flow from within him" (John 7:38). He repeated and confirmed His intentions in John 4:14, namely that whoever drinks this living water will never thirst and it will become "a spring of water welling up to eternal life." The "spring of water welling up to eternal life" is the "water of life" (Rev 22:17) and the very "streams of living water" noted in John 7:38. The words "will flow" are written in future tense because this action will happen in the future.

The Apostle John explained, in verse 38, that "streams of living water" is "the Spirit, whom those who believed in Jesus were later to receive." John's words, "later to receive" make it clear that the Spirit has not been given to them yet. Among the many phrases that add support to his words in the Gospel of John are:

> And I will ask for the Father, and he will give you another Counselor to be with you forever—the Spirit of truth. The world cannot accept him, because it neither sees him nor knows him. But you know him, for he lives with you and will be in you. (John14:16–17)

> But the Counselor, the Holy Spirit, whom the Father will send in my name, will teach you all things and will remind you of everything I have said to you. (John 14:26)

> When the Counselor comes, whom I will send to you from the Father, the Spirit of truth who goes out from the Father, he will testify about me. (John 15:26)

> But I tell you the truth: it is for your good that I am going away. Unless I go away, the Counselor will not come to you; but if I go, I will send him to you. (John 16:7)

Please note that all of the above phrases are written in the future tense. Similarly, let us look at what is written in the book of Luke.

> I am going to send you what my Father has promised; but stay in the city until you have been clothed with power from on high" (Luke 24:49)

> For John baptized with water, but in a few days you will be baptized with the Holy Spirit. (Acts 1:5)

> But you will receive power when the Holy Spirit comes on you; and you will be my witnesses in Jerusalem, and in all Judea and Samaria, and to the ends of the earth. (Acts 1:8)

As you can see, the above verses are also written in the future tense. Clearly, the Holy Spirit had not been sent at the time Jesus spoke these words. Is it true, however, that the Holy Spirit did not exist before now? No, it is not true! The Holy Spirit has existed from the beginning. From reading the Old Testament, we know that the Holy Spirit, using various titles, has been working since the creation of the world. He has been working from the beginning of the New Testament, too. Please refer to the following verses:

- The birth of John the Baptist (Luke 1:15)
- The birth of Jesus (Matt 1:20; Luke 1:35)
- Elizabeth, relative of Maria (Luke 1:41)
- Zechariah, father of John the Baptist (Luke 1:67)
- Simeon (Luke 2:25–27)
- Baptism of Jesus (Matt 3:16–17; Mark 1:9–11; Luke 3:21–22; John 1:32–34)
- Jesus in the desert (Mark 1:12; Luke 4:1)
- Jesus returning to Galilee (Luke 4:14)

- Jesus, full of joy (Luke 10:21)
- Jesus driving out demons (Matt 12:28; Luke 11:20)
- Shedding the blood of Jesus (Heb 9:14)
- Raised Jesus from the dead (Rom 8:11)

But the Apostle John clearly wrote that the Holy Spirit had not been given. Then, are there two Holy Spirits?

One pastor in Burkina Faso, West Africa who studied in the U.K. told me that he has learned there are two Holy Spirits. Of course, this is a matter the professor must qualify, but it might be a mistake to teach this unless he meditates deeply on the Bible.

Could there be two Holy Spirits? No! There is only one Holy Spirit (1 Cor 12:13; Eph 2:18, 4:4)! It only seems like there are two due to "the double works of the Holy Spirit", and these double works started when the Counselor arrived at Pentecost. For better understanding, I would like to divide these teachings into two parts, namely the "outer works of the Holy Spirit" and the "inner works of the Holy Spirit."

First, the outer works of the Holy Spirit are given to people that God chooses whenever necessary in order to do "works" that He wants. It is common knowledge that the Lord used all of the prophets and apostles such as Moses, Joshua, Samson, Gideon, Samuel, David, Solomon, Peter, John, and Paul by pouring the power of the Holy Spirit on them. Our eyes can see these types of outer works by the Holy Spirit as physical changes take place, but the changes are merely temporary.

In the book of Judges, we are told that the Spirit of the Lord came upon Samson in power (13:25; 14:6, 19; 15:14), and also that he was unaware that the Lord had left him. (16:20). In verse 20, "the Lord" means "the Spirit of the Lord" indicating that the Spirit of the Lord can come over someone and then leave. The same words are found in 1 Samuel 16:14: "the Spirit of the Lord had departed from Saul."

When necessary, the Spirit comes but, when no longer needed, leaves. After sinning, David knew that he would be nothing if the Spirit chose to leave. For this reason, he cried out, "Do not cast me from your presence or take your Holy Spirit from me" (Ps 51:11).

The book of Hebrews adds credence to this train of thought with the very fearful words:

> It is impossible for those who have once been enlightened, who have tasted the heavenly gift, who have shared in the Holy Spirit, who have tasted the goodness of the Word of God and the powers of the coming age, if they fall away, to be brought back to repentance, because to their loss they are crucifying the Son of God all over again and subjecting him to public disgrace. (Heb 6:4–6)

> If we deliberately keep on sinning after we have received the knowledge of the truth, no sacrifice for sins is left, but only a fearful expectation of judgment and of raging fire that will consume the enemies of God. Anyone who rejected the law of Moses died without mercy on the testimony of two or three witnesses. How much more severely do you think a man deserves to be punished who has trampled the Son of God under foot, who has treated as an unholy thing the blood of the covenant that sanctified him, and who has insulted the Spirit of grace? For we know him who said, 'It is mine to avenge; I will repay,' and again, 'The Lord will judge his people.' It is a dreadful thing to fall into the hands of the living God. (Heb 10:26–31)

The above words generate heated arguments among theologians and pastors. The problem surfaces when attention is focused on the words, "even you are saved, you can be lost." The Scriptures from Hebrews relate to the double works of the Holy Spirit and are not related to salvation. Let me state unequivocally, once you are saved, you will never lose your salvation! "Who shall separate us from the love of Christ" (Rom 8:35)? Once the Counselor, the Spirit, comes into us, He stays with us forever (John 14:16). Those who say salvation can be lost, in reality have never been saved. They are living on the supposition or with the illusion that they are saved.

So then, what do the above words mean? It is my contention that they speak of the corruption of servants who perform wonderful miracles through the powers of the outer works of the Holy Spirit, and then fall away. If the servants who perform powerful works by the Holy Spirit fall away, this is an insult to the Spirit of grace and is blasphemy against the Holy Spirit (Matt 12:31; Mark 3:29; Luke 12:10). These people can never be saved.

Therefore, any servant of the Lord who executes many miraculous signs and wonders should not seek only the outer works of the Spirit, but should humble, test and examine himself as to whether he is in Christ or not (2 Cor 13:5). I repeat, he must examine himself and make sure that he is saved. Nevertheless, if he carries out powers of the Holy Spirit for his own profit, our Lord will say, "I never knew you. Away from me, you evildoers" (Matt 7:23)!

In the two-thousand-year history of Christianity, how many servants of the Lord turn to corruption once they find success through the power of the Holy Spirit? It is important to note that many are not corrupt in the beginning. At first, they attend church earnestly and devote themselves to church activities. Later, when the power of the Holy Spirit comes upon them, they give of themselves and render offerings only to appropriate power and money for their own use. Many fall away after tasting the heavenly gifts shared by the Holy Spirit.

The outer works of the Holy Spirit are a manifestation of the Spirit (spiritual gift) and given to each person completely according to God's will (1 Cor 12:4–11). So, it is advisable that we do our best to display all of the talents and gifts given to us from the Spirit of God, and that we work to fully develop them. There are some gifts, however, that are determined by the Lord that cannot be developed, including those mentioned in 1 Corinthians 12:4–11:

> There are different kinds of gifts, but the same Spirit. There are different kinds of service, but the same Lord. There are different kinds of working, but the same God works all of them in all men. Now to each one the manifestation of the Spirit is given for the common good. To one there is given through the Spirit the message of wisdom, to another the message of knowledge by means of the same Spirit, to another faith by the same Spirit, to another gifts of healing by that one Spirit, to another miraculous powers, to another prophecy, to another distinguishing between spirits, to another speaking in different kinds of tongues, and to still another the interpretation of tongues. All these are the work of one and the same Spirit, and he gives them to each one, just as he determines.

Some theologians insist that since Pentecost there are no more manifestations of the Holy Spirit. It is my belief that the Holy Spirit is prevailing all over the world through His servants. Either way, please keep in mind that we need such spiritual gifts in this world only.

Another thing to remember is that the outer works of the Holy Spirit have nothing to do with salvation. Therefore, we must carefully use the phrase "experience of the Holy Spirit," which is widely known in the Korean Christian world, or not use the phrase at all. These words may leave the false impression that one is saved as a result of experiencing an outer work of the Holy Spirit. For example, some Pentecostal churches profess that those who speak in tongues are saved. The statement is true in some cases and false in others. Those who are saved may speak in tongues and may receive the gift of tongues when they are baptized with the Holy Spirit (Acts 10:44–46, 19:6). However, not all who speak in tongues are saved and not all who are saved speak in tongues (1 Cor 12:30).

Second, the inner works of the Holy Spirit are those not necessarily visible from the outside, but changes that occur invisibly within the heart. The changes are qualitative—impacting the quality of life—and can be compared to the chemical change of changing water into wine. The sinner changes into a righteous being. Once the inner works of the Holy Spirit change us, the result continues forever (John 14:16). The inner works of the Holy Spirit do not happen as a result of personal power or efforts; they are a gift given totally by the grace of God (Eph 2:8–9).

This inner works of the Holy Spirit are akin to the "baptism of the Holy Spirit," "born again with the Holy Spirit," "sealing with the Holy Spirit," and "salvation." Second, the inner works of the Holy Spirit appear as "the fruit of the Holy Spirit" as presented in Galatians 5:22–23:

> But the fruit of the Spirit is love, joy, peace, patience, kindness, goodness, faithfulness, gentleness and self-control. Against such things there is no law.

The fruit of the Holy Spirit is the very character of the Holy Spirit, the very character of Jesus, and also the very character of God. Therefore, we need the experience of the inner works of the Holy Spirit first and then are to eagerly desire the outer works of the Holy Spirit—spiritual gifts (1 Cor 12:31; 14:1, 39).

The outer works and the inner works of the Holy Spirit can happen at the same time, just as they did at Pentecost. The Apostle Paul describe the double works of the Holy Spirit in 1 Corinthians 12:4–13 as follows:

> There are different kinds of gifts, but the same Spirit. There are different kinds of service, but the same Lord. There are different kinds of working, but the same God works all of them in all men. Now to each one the manifestation of the Spirit is given for the common good. To one there is given through the Spirit the message of wisdom, to another the message of knowledge by means of the same Spirit, to another faith by the same Spirit, to another gifts of healing by the same Spirit, to another miraculous powers, to another prophecy, to another distinguishing between spirits, to another speaking in different kinds of tongues, and to still another the interpretation of the tongues. All these are the work of one and the same Spirit, and he gives them to each one, just as he determines. The body is a unit, though it is made up of many parts; and though all its parts are many, they form one body. So it is with Christ. For we were all baptized by one Spirit into one body—whether Jews or Greeks, slave or free—and we were all given the one Spirit to drink.

In the above phrases, why do you think the gifts are described differently as the Spirit (verse 4), the Lord (verse 5), and God (verse 6)? The works of the Trinity of God are apparent in that "the Lord" represents "Jesus the Son of God" and "God" represents "God the Father." The concept is even easier to understand by substituting "Spirit" for both "the Lord" and "God," so the passage reads, "one and the same Spirit." This can be done because the Holy Spirit is the Lord and God, too. Actually the Holy Spirit gives not only gifts to the saints, but also allows them to serve and work, notably in evangelism and missions.

According to verses 4 through 11, the outer works of the Holy Spirit, are given not to everyone but to whom the Holy Spirit determines. The gifts are not related to salvation, they do not employ miraculous powers, nor do they afford the ability to speak in tongues—even though the person is saved. Scripture asks, "Do all have gifts of healing? Do all speak in tongues" (1 Cor 12:30)? The answer is "no" even though it is clear that believers have received the baptism of the Holy Spirit, the inner works of the Holy Spirit, through which we become "one body," that is, "the body of Jesus Christ." Once again, this is salvation!

The following chart illustrates the outer and inner works of the Holy Spirit:

Outer Works	Inner Works
Physical change (water/ice)	Chemical change (water/wine)
Visible outside (healing, etc.)	Change inside (salvation)
Temporary (Judg 16:20; Ps 51:11)	Permanent (John 14:16)
Spirit determines (1 Cor 12:11)	God's grace (Eph 2:8–9)
Given as needed	Given one time
Manifestation of the Spirit	Fruit of the Spirit
Need in the world only	Need in the world and heaven

"The streams of living water" as described by the Lord Jesus in John 7:38, mean solely that the "Counselor, the Holy Spirit," comes in "the name of Jesus," who came down at Pentecost for the first time. Please know that the double works of the Holy Spirit continue at the present time. It is with great joy and anticipation that we are able to watch, experience, and observe them within ourselves and in others.

14

The Fruit of the Holy Spirit

"But the fruit of the Spirit is love, joy, peace, patience, kindness, goodness, faithfulness, gentleness and self-control" (Gal 5:22–23). We all know the above words well, but I would like to delve deeper into their meaning in this chapter. For those who long to study the subject in greater detail, I would recommend other books with an emphasis in pneumatology.

When we are baptized with the Holy Spirit, the first phenomenon we experience is the fruit of the Holy Spirit. Our hearts are full of love, joy, peace, etc. The word "fruit" is singular to denote that the nine different characteristics of the Holy Spirit are given at one time. If love is apparent but there is no joy, or if joy is expressed but there is no peace in the heart, then we are not in the fullness of the Holy Spirit and our natural character is revealed.

Some theologians classify the nine characters of the fruit of the Holy Spirit into the following three parts:

- Love, joy, peace, which are related with himself
- Patience, kindness, goodness, which are related with his neighbor
- Faithfulness, gentleness, self-control, which are related with God

As we can see, the first phenomena appearing to a believer when he is baptized with the Holy Spirit are love, joy, and peace. Our Lord Jesus commanded that we "be filled with the Spirit" in Ephesians 5:18, which means that all of the fruit of the Holy Spirit and the inner fullness of the Holy Spirit comes over us. In the Bible, there are many references to fruit, such as "the fruit of the light" (Eph 5:9) and "the fruit of righteousness" (Phil 1:11), but the ultimate fruit is the fruit of the Holy Spirit.

Looking at the nine characteristics of the fruit of the Spirit, it would be wise to examine ourselves as to whether we are experiencing the fullness of the Holy Spirit. Within this pursuit, 1 Corinthians 13 offers a definition of love and every characteristic of love should be apparent at the same time when you are in love. By meditating on God's Word day and night (Ps 1:2, 119:97), praying fervently (Eph 6:18; Jude 20), and building close fellowship with the Holy Spirit, we are able to live victoriously in this endeavor.

> Love is patient, love is kind. It does not envy, it does not boast, it is not proud. It is not rude, it is not self-seeking, it is not easily angered, it keeps no record of wrongs. Love does not delight in evil, but rejoices with the truth. It always protects, always trusts, always hopes, always perseveres. (1 Corinthians 13:4–7)

I genuinely hope that all of you exude the very image of Jesus, bearing the full fruit of the Holy Spirit through the fullness of the Holy Spirit.

15

The Spiritual Gifts of the Holy Spirit

For the sake of simplicity, we are studying various aspects of the gifts of the Holy Spirit in separate chapters. In chapters 13 and 14, respectively, we examined the double works of the Holy Spirit and the fruit of the Spirit. Detailed information can also be found in other books on pneumatology. In this chapter, I would like to explore some additional points concerning spiritual gifts.

Among nine spiritual gifts, "the gift of the message of knowledge" (1 Cor 12:8) allows the Spirit who searches all things—even the deep things and thoughts of God (1 Cor 2:10–11)—to gain a portion of His knowledge. In 2 Kings 6:8–12 for example, the Prophet Elisha informs the King of Israel about every movement the Arameans make, which allows them to be victorious whenever they go into battle. This is a case where the Holy Spirit gives a part of His knowledge to the Prophet Elisha.

"The message of wisdom" (1 Cor 12:8) as given by the Holy Spirit provides us with part of His wisdom. In 1 Kings 3, King Solomon judges wisely because he has wisdom from God (1 Kgs 3:28), even though he does not know facts about the two women in question. This is the gift of the Holy Spirit, who is also "the Spirit of wisdom and understanding" (Isa 11:2).

Speaking in tongues is one of the spiritual gifts and also a "sign accompanying those who believe in the name of Jesus" (Mark 16:17–18). If we consider that faith is also one of the spiritual gifts, "the sign of believing" (miracles) is also certainly one of the spiritual gifts of the Holy Spirit.

There is much doctrinal division concerning the gift of tongues. First of all, no one understands the language of tongues because the Holy Spirit enables a person's language, or tongue, to utter mysteries with their spirit (Acts 2:4; 1 Cor 14:2). Some people say that when they speak foreign languages that they do not otherwise know, they are speaking in tongues. However, if others recognize the words as a foreign language, this is not tongues as described in the Bible since it says that no one understands tongues. Quoting from Acts 2, when people from various countries gathered together and heard the same Gospel message each in their own tongue, an acquaintance of mine insists that because many people understood the tongues in their own native languages, the disciples are speaking foreign languages as tongues. This assessment disagrees with the Bible.

I believe that the people who understood the tongues as their native language received the gift of the *interpretation* of tongues. Scripture also says that some in attendance made fun of those speaking in tongues, thinking they have had too much wine (Acts 2:13). For sure, these people did not receive the gift of the interpretation of tongues.

It is my contention that even if each of the one hundred twenty disciples spoke a different foreign language, they would have had great difficulty trying to understand even their own language since they were all speaking at the same time. In addition, the Bible says that if anyone speaks in a tongue, someone must interpret (1 Cor 14:27). If, however, someone speaks in a *foreign* language that is understood by others, the Bible does not require that an interpreter translate because this is not a tongue.

In accordance with the Lord's command, believers are encouraged to eagerly desire not only the greater spiritual gifts, but also the gift of tongues (1 Cor 12:31, 14:1). The Bible clearly states that speaking in tongues is not forbidden (1 Cor 14:39). The Apostle Paul gave thanks to God for granting him the ability to speak in tongues to more than all the saints in the Corinthian church (1 Cor 14:18). Scripturally speaking, if someone speaks in tongues within the church, an interpreter is required (1 Cor 14:27). If there is no interpreter, I recommend praying privately in tongues in order to strengthen your spirit and edify yourself (1 Cor 14:4, 14).

As our discussion shifts to the study of prophecy, I would like to point out that originally, the purpose of prophecy was "to tell what is yet to come" (John 16:13). The Bible teaches that "the Word of God" is also "prophecy" (2 Pet 1:21; Rev 1:2–3). Because, almost every "Word of God" is "prophecy" about "things yet to come," much of the prophecy has been fulfilled. Why then does our Lord ask us to eagerly desire "the gift of prophecy" among "the greater gifts" (1 Cor 12:31, 14:1)?

All words proclaiming the Christian faith are prophecy and all prophecy will absolutely be fulfilled. Scripture teaches believers to build our faith because faith is being sure of what we hope for and certain of what we do not see (Heb 11:1). When it comes to professing faith, the power of *our word* is as powerful as the *Word of God*, according to the Hebraic (*dabar*) and Greek (*logos*) definitions of "Word." Both mean "the Word of God" and "the word of men." For this reason, the Lord said, "As surely as I live, declares the Lord, I will do to you the very things I heard you say" (Num 14:28). He also said, "Open wide your mouth and I will fill it" (Ps 81:10) because He created our mouth and lips (Exod 4:11; Isa 57:19).

Thus, all the words we proclaim with faith through the Holy Spirit for the church, members of the congregation, and our children become prophecy through which all receive great blessing. Prophecy edifies church members by offering them strength, encouragement, and comfort. (1 Cor 14:3–6). These are a few of the reasons the Lord asks believers to eagerly desire prophecy (1 Cor 14:1, 39)

In summary, I would like to encourage believers to speak continuously in tongues, interpret these tongues, and prophesy once such gifts are received. In 1 Corinthians chapter 14, the Lord instructs us how to use these three among the nine spiritual gifts. The most important spiritual gift to desire is to follow the way of love (1 Cor 14:1) because we are nothing in spite of how many spiritual gifts we have, unless we have love (1 Cor 13:1–3). This section of Scripture is deemed the love chapter and love is the first characteristic of the fruit of the Holy Spirit. Therefore, once we are filled with the Holy Spirit, it is good and right that we desire spiritual gifts, including the outer works of the Holy Spirit and the inner works of the Holy Spirit.

As spiritual gifts are the manifestation of the Holy Spirit, this is also a very suitable way for the Holy Spirit to manifest Himself to us and to express His love for us.

I do hope all of you have authentic and successful church lives with the help of the Holy Spirit!

16

The Fullness of the Holy Spirit

TWO KINDS of "fullness of the Holy Spirit" are found in the Bible. One is written, "filled with the Holy Spirit" and the other, "full of the Holy Spirit." In the Greek, "filled with" is *pleetho* in verb form and "full of" is *pleerees* in noun form.

Filled with—*pleetho*—means that the Holy Spirit comes upon from the outside to fill. This coming upon from the outside indicates "the outer works of the Holy Spirit."

Full of—*pleerees*—means that the Holy Spirit flows from the inside in order to make full, which denotes "the inner works of the Holy Spirit."

In cases of outer fullness, gifts of the Holy Spirit can be seen outwardly whereas, in cases of the inner fullness, a believer's heart is full of the Holy Spirit and gifts are manifested as the fruit of the Holy Spirit (i.e. peace, love, joy, kindness, forgiveness, self-control, etc.).

When the Apostle Peter preached the Gospel of being "filled with the Holy Spirit," about three thousand people were converted to faith, baptized, and saved (Acts 2:14–41). Later, when Deacon Stephen preached the Gospel of being "full of the Holy Spirit," the crowd did not repent and, instead, stoned and killed him (Acts 7:54–60).

The fullness of the Holy Spirit as offered by Peter offered the outer works of the Holy Spirit, including such things as the message of wisdom and the message of knowledge. The power of the Holy Spirit moved people to repent and they were saved. Stephen's case, on the other hand, presented the inner works of the Holy Spirit. His power to forgive the crowd as they stoned him to death was the outcome of the fruit of the Holy Spirit.

In the New Testament, there are two places where "the inner fullness of the Holy Spirit" is written as the verb "filled with." In Acts 13:52, it is written, "And the disciples were filled with joy and with the Holy Spirit" and in Ephesians 5:18, "Instead, be filled with the Spirit." This use of "filled with" is the Greek *pleeroo* as a verb, which is derived from the Greek noun *pleerees* indicating "inner fullness of the Holy Spirit." It is for this reason the English Bible employs the same verb "filled with."

Therefore, "filled with joy" (Acts 13:52) is one of the character traits of the fruit of the Holy Spirit that results from the "inner fullness of the Holy Spirit." Similarly, to "be filled with the Spirit" (Eph 5:18) as commanded by the Lord, calls upon believers to have the "inner fullness of the Holy Spirit" in order to live a successful church life full of the fruit of the Holy Spirit. What we do with our will is not the outer fullness of the Holy Spirit but the inner fullness of the Holy Spirit. Contrarily, spiritual gifts as the outer fullness of the Holy Spirit will not be given according to our will but according to the will of the Holy Spirit.

Although believers are encouraged to desire the greater spiritual gifts, it is more important to align our will with the Word of God in order to have the inner fullness of the Holy Spirit bearing the fruit of the Holy Spirit. When we are full of the Holy Spirit, the fruit of the Holy Spirit is fully born within the heart, and a likeness to Jesus and the image of God is apparent within us.

The phrases "filled with" and "full of" appear in the following verses:

- Filled with (outer fullness): Luke 1:15, 41, 67; Acts 2:4; 4:8, 31; 9:17, 13:9
- Full of (inner fullness): Luke 4:1; Acts 6:3, 5; 7:55; 11:24

The best way to have the fullness of the Holy Spirit is simply to listen to what the Holy Spirit says (Rev 2, 3). The voice of the Holy Spirit is the very voice of God and Jesus. God's voice is the written Word. The Holy Spirit speaks in the form of dreams, visions, and through others. According to the Word of God, what we believe and how we live is actually a reflection of the way in which we respond to the voice of the Holy Spirit. This is so because the Holy Spirit is the author of the Word of God and the Word Himself. When we pattern our life by the voice of God and the Holy Spirit, the Holy Spirit will fully dwell within us and give us the power needed to accomplish the will of the Lord.

My hope for each of you is that are successful in everyday life with the fullness of the Holy Spirit who gives the fruit of the Holy Spirit and power!

17

All the Works of the Holy Spirit

IN THIS chapter, I would like to demonstrate how the outer and inner works of the Holy Spirit—as written in the Bible—control every activity in nature, including human beings and our family and church lives.

The following list of Scriptures is a sampling of this concept:

1. Testifies about Jesus (evangelization and mission): John 15:26–27; Acts 1:8; 4:8, 31; 5:32; 6:10; 13:2, 4; 20:28; Rev 22:17
2. Testifies to us as God's children: Rom 8:16; Gal 4:6
3. Allows us to be born again: John 3:5–7; Titus 3:5
4. Teaches and reminds: John 14:26; Luke 12:12; Acts 8:29, 10:19, 13:2; 1 Cor 2:13
5. Gives power (Job 33:4, 34:14–15; Pss 33:6, 104:30; Isa 40:7; Luke 1:35; Acts 1:8)
6. Gives resurrection (Rom 8:11)
7. Helps and intercedes for us (Rom 8:26–27)
8. Guides us into all truth—Jesus (John 16:13)
9. Brings glory to Jesus (John 16:14)
10. Convicts the world of guilt (John 16:8)
11. Gives spiritual gifts (1 Cor 12:8–12)
12. Bears fruit (Gal 5:22–23)

All the Works of the Holy Spirit 105

13. Makes holy (1 Cor 6:11; 2 Thess 2:13; 1 Pet 1:2)
14. Guards and shields (2 Tim 1:14; 1 Pet 1:5)
15. Makes one (1 Cor 12:13; Eph 4:3)
16. Overflows with hope (Rom 15:13)
17. Strengthens our inner being (Eph 3:16)
18. Gives freedom (2 Cor 3:17)
19. Gives wisdom and knowledge (Exod 31:3–5)
20. Calls us to worship (Phil 3:3)
21. Makes fellowship (2 Cor 13:13; Phil 2:1)
22. Encourages (Acts 9:31)
23. Revives the church (Acts 11:21, 24)
24. Compels and warns (Acts 20:22–23)
25. Makes overseers of the church (Acts 20:28)
26. Reveals and searches (1 Cor 2:10)
27. Knows the thoughts of God (1 Cor 2:11)
28. Transforms into God's likeness (2 Cor 3:18)
29. Praises God (Acts 10:46)
30. Gives joy (Luke 10:21; 1 Thess 1:6)
31. Gives prophecy, dreams, and visions (1 Sam 10:6, 10; Joel 2:28; Acts 2:17-18, 11:28; Rev 4:2)
32. Sees the Lord Jesus (Rev 1:10–16)
33. Falls as dead (Rev 1:17)
34. Moves to another place (1 Kgs 18:12; Ezek 3:14, 8:3, 11:1, 37:1; Acts 8:39)
35. Moves us to keep the laws (Ezek 36:27)
36. Instructs (Acts 1:2)
37. Calls Jesus as Lord (1 Cor 12:3)
38. Conceives the Christ child (Matt 1:20; Luke 1:35; Gal 4:29)
39. Renews (Titus 3:5)
40. Speaks in crisis (Matt 10:20; Luke 12:12)

41. Drives out demons (Matt 12:28; Luke 11:20)
42. Gives life (John 3:6; Rom 8:2; 2 Cor 3:6)
43. Sheds the blood of Jesus (Heb 9:14)
44. Moves the heart (Judg 13:25, 14:6; 1 Chr 12:18; 2 Chr 24:20)
45. Gathers the scroll of the Lord (Isa 34:16)
46. Writes Scripture (2 Tim 3:16; 2 Pet 1:21)

Of course there are many other Scriptures that explain actions carried out by the Holy Spirit. Numerous passages are cited in chapter 5, "*Other Titles of the Holy Spirit.*"

In addition to the above list of actions, if consideration is given to being "touched, incited, and moved by God or the Lord," there are many citations in the Old Testament (1 Sam 10:26; 2 Sam 24:1; 2 Chr 36:22). In the New Testament, references to "the Lord" (Acts 2:47) as "the Holy Spirit" are understood to be actions carried out by the Holy Spirit.

The most important and frequently used words with regard to church life are faith, hope, and love. While in this world, the three most important activities for saints to engage in are:

1. Upward activities toward God such as worship and praise
2. Inward activities such as loving fellowship and learning the Word of God
3. Outward activities such as evangelization and mission work

Do you think all those activities are possible without help from the Holy Spirit? Nothing is possible without the Holy Spirit! Even the Word of God would not exist without the Holy Spirit!

There are some interesting stories in the Bible that relate how the Holy Spirit works even when the name of the Holy Spirit is not mentioned. For example:

> All the people in the synagogue were furious when they heard this. They got up, drove him out of the town, and took him on the brow of the hill on which the town was built, in order to throw him down the cliff. But he walked right through the crowd and went on his way. (Luke 4:28–30)

> When they had rowed three or three and a half miles, they saw Jesus approaching the boat, walking on the water; and they were terrified. But he said to them, 'It is I; don't be afraid.' Then they were willing to take him into the boat, and immediately the boat reached the shore where they were heading. (John 6:19–21)

> When Jesus said, 'I am he,' they drew back and fell to the ground. (John 18:6)

The actions mentioned, "he walked right through the crowd," "walking on the water," "immediately the boat reached the shore," and "they drew back and fell to the ground" can only be accomplished through the power of the Holy Spirit—though the Holy Spirit is not mentioned.

Please keep in mind that everything that happens in the universe, in the world, and in our daily lives is being done through the Holy Spirit, the Spirit of the Sovereign Lord!

18

The Name of the Holy Spirit

THE NAME of the Holy Spirit is very important to the doctrine of the Holy Spirit. This is a different viewpoint from *Other Titles of the Holy Spirit* as explored in chapter 5.

Every person on earth has their own name because they are individual people. Our name represents our person, our personality, and our face. In the present day and age it is possible to get lots of information about a person by conducting searches on a computer. All kinds of data can be found, such as birthplace, educational background, career, address, family status, and more.

Having a name is required by the government in order to create necessary documents. Having a name is essential for enrolling in school or getting a job. Carrying a passport with name and photo is needed for international travel. Possessing a name is required in order to open a bank account, make a deposit, or withdraw funds. Indeed, our name must be written in the book of life in the kingdom of heaven, too! Having a name is extremely important; no one can live without one.

Recently, a movie hit on this very subject, though I don't know whether it was based on a true story or not. One day the leading actor went to the bank to draw out money. After giving his name, the teller told him there was no one by that name in the computer. Although he insisted his name should be in the computer, the teller refused to accommodate him, saying it wasn't there. Getting nowhere, the man went to another branch of the bank. There, he was given the same answer. Finally he went to the resident registration office. The official put his name into the computer and announced that this person was dead. The man countered that this was his name and he was very much alive. His efforts were of no use because the computer listed him as dead. In distress, he committed suicide. The movie may have been filmed to point out the error of accepting that computers are always right, but it also underscores the importance of a name.

Every name has meaning, especially those of Koreans and Israelites. For example, "Joseph" stands for "God will add" and "Daniel" as "God is my judge." Normally the parents, and primarily the father, assign a name and hope the child grows to become like a specific person having the same name. In America and Europe, this is why many parents of the Christian tradition name their children after people in the Bible. They pray that their child grows to become like the one that bears his namesake.

Names are considered valuable and people appreciate when others remember a name. They are happy when their child's name is well known, honored, and exalted. In some cultures, if a child makes a mistake, the father is blamed. Being upset, the father then rebukes the child and, in some cases, drives the child out of his house because the child brought dishonor to the father's name.

People have been known to risk life and limb for the sake of their name, or to preserve honor within the family, because the name of a person represents who he is.

There are many who desire to leave their name for posterity, to be famous, or be much revered. Koreans especially want to leave their names forever. This pattern can be observed throughout the many tourist draws in Europe. Whenever I visit the castle of Heidelberg about one hundred kilometers south of Frankfurt, Germany, where I live, I see lots of names written on the walls and tables. There are more Korean names written here than any other nationality. Recently, all the walls were painted white and in just a few short days, names began to appear on the walls again. A familiar proverb in Korea states that "A tiger dies but its skin remains and a man dies but his name remains," and sometimes Koreans say, "Please pray for your name!" People consider their names to be of great worth.

To be honest, our Lord God considers His name to be even more valuable because he is a person Himself and He has His own name. I would like to explain in due course why God considers His name to hold such value.

The word "name" can be found very often in the Bible, especially in the Old Testament. Among them, "the name of God," "the name of the Lord," "the name of the Lord Almighty," "the Lord's name," "my name," and "my holy name" are found frequently. The *Christian Dictionary* published in Korea defines "the name of God" as follows:

> In the Bible, the name of God is an essential element in order to understand God. The name shows His original nature and His personal character. When people introduce him to others, he must tell his name first. Likewise, the Self-Revelation of God is related to the fact that He informs His Name to His people first, and then His people will know Him and worship Him. Accordingly, the name of God represents the personal relationship between God and His people, and also reveals His authority and presence. The most important one among the Name of God in the Old Testament is 'Jehovah'

as Covenanted Name and 'El', 'Elohim' and 'Eloah' as general Name.[1]

Strictly speaking, *El* or *Elohim* are not names of God because *El* means God as a singular noun and *Elohim* means God as a plural noun in general, not "the name of God." "Jehovah" (*YHWH*) is the only personal name of God. The Lord told Moses that He is "I AM WHO I AM" (Exod 3:14) and His name as *YHWH* (Exod 6:3, 15:3, 34:5–6).

Normally when people meet other people, proper etiquette dictates that they exchange names. Conversation is generally more relaxed and better understood once people get to know one another's names and backgrounds. Therefore, Moses asked the name of God and he surely wanted himself to know the name of God.

On the other hand, God might have been embarrassed when Moses asked His name, considering God's exalted position. Traditionally, the exchange of names occurs between those of equal or similar status, and here, Moses asked the name of the Creator, God! But God kindly told Moses His name, "I AM WHO I AM." Please note that all of the letters are capitalized. In English grammar, "I" is the subject and the word that follows, "am" should be the verb, but in this phrase, "I AM" is the subject and "WHO I AM" becomes a complement. How can God, the Creator, give His name to His created people?

I believe that the Korean translation of "I AM WHO I AM" as "the Self-Being" is rather smart. Because the original Hebrew of "I AM WHO I AM" stems from *haya* or "*hawa*," ancient words meaning "existence," they hold the same meaning as the verb "be" in English. From these words came the name of God, *YHWH,* which is incredibly precise because there is only One God, the Creator who is the only "Self-Being" in this universe!

1. Han, Yung-je, *The Dictionary of Christianity*, 1013.

However, the Israelites would not dare call *YHWH* the name of God. They called Him *Adonai* instead. *Adonai* actually means "the Lord," not "the name of God." Only *YHWH* has been given to the Israelites as "the name of God," in connection with the covenant made between God and the people of Israel. In other words, God, who is "The Self-Being," has given the name *YHWH* for the purpose of carrying out His covenant with Israel.

The Israelites identified *YHWH Rapha* as "the Lord who heals" (Exod 15:26), *YHWH Nes* as "the Lord is my banner" (Exod 17:15), and *YHWH Shalom* as "the Lord is peace" (Judg 6:24). There is, of course, no mention of *YHWH* in the New Testament because it is a Greek word. We can only find "God" and *kurios,* the Greek word for "Lord" which is translated from the Hebrew *Adonai*.

However, praise God, in the era of the New Testament, the Lord our God gave us the wonderful and glorious name that is above every name (Phil 2:9), and that is the very name of "Jesus!"

God the Father sent His Son, who is Immanuel, to us in order to be with us and He gave Him the name "Jesus" (Matt 1:23, 25). As mentioned before, a father gives a name to his son along with his hopes and wishes for the future. The name of "Jesus," of course, is the name of "the Son of God" or "God the Son." The New Testament makes it clear in the Trinity of God and reveals that the name of this person in the Trinity is "Jesus!"

After being raised from the dead, God the Son commanded His disciples to go and make disciples of all nations, baptizing them in the name of the Father, of the Son and of the Holy Spirit (Matt 28:19). Their main purpose is to make disciples of all nations but they have to "baptize in the name of the Father, of the Son and of the Holy Spirit" in order to make them disciples. Therefore, all the churches in the world baptize in the name of the Father, of the Son, and of the Holy Spirit. I don't mean that it is wrong. But the intention of the command of the Lord is to "baptize in the name of the Father, in the name of the Son, and in the name of the Holy Spirit." This means to baptize *calling the name* of the Father, the *name* of the Son and the *name* of the Holy Spirit! The problem is in baptizing without "calling on the name." We should remember that the Apostle Paul was baptized calling on the name of Jesus (Acts 22:16).

For example, if the president of a country nominates members of the Cabinet, he nominates "in the name of the president of the country." In that case, the actual name of the president along with his title is included in the letter of appointment. Otherwise, it is unfinished. For instance in the United States, "President George W. Bush" would be written in combination with "the President of the United States of America." To simply say "the name of the president of the United States of America" without actually stating the name is not enough. It is invalid.

It is clear to that "the name of the Son" is "Jesus" but many pastors might not understand exactly "the name of the Father" and "the name of the Holy Spirit." This is why most baptize "in the name of the Father, of the Son, and of the Holy Spirit."

The best way to determine what to say during baptism is to open the Bible to the book of Acts and witness how the disciples followed Jesus' command to baptize. Next, we look at the Gospel of John and read what the Apostle John wrote about the name of God.

First, we will discover phrases the disciples used about baptism:

> Peter replied, 'Repent and be baptized, every one of you, in the name of Jesus Christ for the forgiveness of your sins. And you will receive the gift of the Holy Spirit.' (Acts 2:38)

> because the Holy Spirit had not yet come upon any of them; they had simply been baptized into the name of the Lord Jesus. (Acts 8:16)
>
> So he ordered that they be baptized in the name of Jesus Christ. (Acts 10:48a)

The Apostle Paul also baptized disciples of the church in Ephesus using the name of the Lord Jesus (Acts 19:5), as he himself was also baptized in the name of Jesus (Acts 22:16).

The disciples of Jesus faithfully obeyed the commandment of the Lord and baptized "in the name of Jesus Christ" or "into the name of the Lord Jesus." They did this because they knew that "Jesus" is not only "the name of the Son," but also "the name of the Father," and "the name of the Holy Spirit."

The Apostle John testifies to the same in his Gospel as well. Jesus Himself, the son of God, stated in John 5:43:

> I have come in my Father's name.

When the Son of God was born in the world, God, the Father, gave the name "Jesus" to His Son through the angel (Matt 1:20–21; Luke 1:30–31; John 17:11–12). And the name "Jesus" is nothing but "the name of the Father" and "the name of the Father" is "Jesus!"

In chapter 17 of the Gospel of John, we see that Jesus, the Son of God, prays to God, the Father, saying, "Holy Father, protect them by the power of your name—the name you gave me—so that they may be one as we are one" (John 17:11b). "The name of Jesus," as given to the Son, is nothing but "the very name of the Father!"

The "name of the Holy Spirit," is also written as "Jesus" in John 14:26:

> But the Counselor, the Holy Spirit, whom the Father will send in my name, will teach you all

things and will remind you of everything I have
said to you.

Jesus says that the Father will send the Counselor, the Holy Spirit, in "His name Jesus," which was given to Him by His Father. For more explanations about "the Counselor, the Holy Spirit," please refer to chapters 11 and 13, *The Holy Spirit and Baptism*" and "*The Double Works of the Holy Spirit.*

I like to explain it simply, by saying that "Jesus" is "the name of the Son of God" and because the Son of God is also "God," "Jesus" is "the name of God," too. This means "Jesus" is the "name of the Trinity of God." Therefore, "Jesus" is "the name of the Father, the name of the Son, and the name of the Holy Spirit!"

I would like to explain why God considers His name, "Jesus" to be so valuable, and why the name of Jesus is so important.

Gordon D. Fee, who is famous for studying the theology of Paul, expressed beautifully in his book *Paul, the Spirit and the People of God*, that what the beloved people most want is "presence together." He shares that "the Holy Spirit" is "the Renewed Presence of God."[2] God, who loves us so much, wants to have a close relationship with us—a relationship that can never be separated under any circumstances. He wants to be with us as one body forever, without separation or the absence of God's love.

Therefore, the Lord God asked Moses to build a tabernacle in order to dwell among the Israelites (Exod 25:8), in which to meet Moses (Exod 25:22), and where He could be with them. Then, God asked King Solomon to build the temple for a different reason. God asked King Solomon to build the temple for "my Name" or for "the Name of the Lord" (1 Kgs 8:17–18; 2 Kgs 23:27; 1 Chr 22:7–10, 19;

---

2. Fee, *Paul, The Spirit and the People of God*, 9.

29:16; 2 Chr 2:4, 6; 6:7–10, 34, 38), and also for "my Name to be there" (1 Kgs 8:16; 2 Chr 6:20). Here is an example from 1 Kings 9:3:

> The Lord said to him: 'I have heard the prayer and plea you have made before me; I have consecrated this temple, which you have built, by putting my Name there forever. My eyes and my heart will always be there.'

But, even though the temple was "for the Name of the Lord" or "with the Name of the Lord" and it was beautiful and costly, it may as well have been destroyed by fire since the Israelites refused to obey the Word of God. In the end, God the Father sent His One and Only Son Jesus to the world as Immanuel in order to make His body as a temple (John 2:21).

The body of Jesus was the temple and, therefore, the temple should also have been destroyed because of His flesh. There is no redemption without shedding blood, no resurrection without death, no ascension without resurrection, no glorification without ascension, no Pentecost without glorification; and then finally the Counselor, the Holy Spirit with "the Name of Jesus" can come down to us after the glorification of Jesus (John 7:39).

Even then Son of God, Jesus, who is Immanuel or "God with us," cannot dwell with us forever, nor give His Name as long as He had flesh. The only way God can dwell with us forever is when "the Counselor, the Holy Spirit with Jesus' Name" comes into us and makes us "the temple of the Holy Spirit." The Bible tells us that the Most High does not live in houses made by men (Acts 7:48, 17:24) even the highest heaven cannot contain (1 Kgs 8:27)! But the Most High wants to dwell with you and I—sinners who are weak like jars of clay! How great is the love of God! The Apostle Paul wrote in 1 Corinthians 6:11:

> But you were washed, you were sanctified, you were justified in the name of the Lord Jesus Christ and by the Spirit of our God.

Using a real-world example, I would like to compare a 400-meter relay race to how the Lord God can give us the name of Jesus. A 400-meter relay team consists of four runners that race as one team. All four runners get gold medals when their team wins. But, even if they finish the race in first place, they must cross the finish line with the baton or they are disqualified. As each runner finishes his leg of the race, he must hand off the baton to the next runner. If a runner drops the baton, he must pick it up before continuing to race.

Concerning the giving of names, some Americans and Europeans continue the legacy of their name by passing it on to a son. To distinguish a father from his son, sometimes the name Jr. (junior) is added. For example, John F. Kennedy, Jr., or R. A. Torrey III (the third). Likewise, God the Father has given to His Son the name "Jesus" and this is the "name of the Father" (Matt 1:21). The Son of God, named "Jesus," ascended to heaven after finishing His work in this world, and giving "the name Jesus" to the "Counselor, the Spirit of truth." After that, "the Counselor, the Holy Spirit who has the name Jesus" can pass "the baton called the name of Jesus" to us. In this way, we will finally have "the name Jesus" within us only after "the Counselor, the Holy Spirit with Jesus name" comes into us. This means the Trinity of God lives in us (Phil 2:13; 1 John 4:12) since the name of the Trinity of God is Jesus, and also means "Christ lives in us" (Rom 8:10; 2 Cor 13:5; Gal 2:20; Phil 1:21) because "Jesus" is Christ and the Holy Spirit is "the Spirit of Christ."

Whenever I explain this part during one of my pastor seminars, I invite four pastors to come to the front of the podium, give one of them my ballpoint pen, and explain how the 400-meter relay race is run. I teach that the first runner is God the Father, the second runner is the Son of God, the third runner is the Holy Spirit, and I "myself" become the fourth runner. Then, we act out the relay. The first runner gives the pen to the second runner, the second runner gives it to the third runner, and the third runner gives it to the fourth runner. This ballpoint pen is "the very name Jesus." After participating in this exercise, most of the pastors understand and are excited at this revelation. Do you know why they are so happy and excited?

The Holy Spirit as the third runner has come to me and let me have the "name of Jesus." Normally, in the 400-meter relay, the fourth runner is the fastest on the team. This means spiritually that *we* are the best runners. When *we* preach the Gospel, *we* are working together with the Trinity of God, the Father, the Son, and the Holy Spirit as one team including *me*. I am the best runner and the most important person among them, and with good reason.

A careful read of chapters 8, 9, and 10 of Acts helps us to understand why. This text teaches that the angels, the Holy Spirit, or Jesus Himself can talk with the people but cannot preach the Gospel by themselves. They have arranged for saints such as Philip, Ananias, and Peter to preach the Gospel and win souls for salvation. Why is it that the Almighty God or angels are unable to preach the Gospel?

There are lots of promises of God in the Bible and most offer rewards, awards, and crowns to be given to the saints according to the works they have done during their lifetime in this world. If anyone gives even a cup of cold water to the little one because he is Jesus' disciple, he will certainly receive his reward (Matt 10:42). If there are no rewards in the kingdom of heaven, God surely would take us up to the kingdom of heaven as soon as we are saved, namely as soon as we are baptized with the Holy Spirit. Also, why would God, the Lord, let us live in this painfully harsh world instead of taking us up to heaven after salvation? Not only does he want us to stay in the world to bear witness to others and help bring them into the kingdom but also, he desires to reward us!

And what do you think is the reward of all reward? Isn't it a single soul, which could not be exchanged for the whole world because the soul is more valuable than the whole world? Even our God the Lord, who loved us so much and dwells within us forever, cannot preach the Gospel because He wants us to earn the crowns and rewards for saving souls. When the pastors realize the wonderful love of God and the fact that even angels, the Holy Spirit, and Jesus can do nothing unless they (the people) preach the Gospel, they are very happy and excited. This is why we have to be the best runner in the race for preaching the Gospel to the ends of the earth—with the Holy Spirit as our master!

There are other reasons why God the Lord has given us the name Jesus, in addition to being with us forever.

- Jesus' name has the power to forgive sins and break the chains of the devil. (Ps 118:10–12; Luke 24:47; Acts 10:43; 1 Cor 6:11; 1 John 2:12)
- Jesus' name gives salvation and eternal life, (Ps 54:1, 79:9, 116:4; Isa 63:16; John 1:12, 20:31; Acts 2:21, 16:31; Rom 10:13; 1 John 5:11–13) and no other name is given to us. (Acts 4:12)
- Jesus' name gives blessings (Num 6:27; Pss 118:26, 129:8; Mal 4:2) and treasures of wisdom and knowledge, (Col 2:3) and it protects us. (Ps 20:1)
- Jesus' name has authority and power (Jer 10:6) because God the Father exalted the name of Jesus far above all rule, authority, and every name. (Eph 1:21; Phil 2:9–11; Heb 1:4)

Therefore, Jesus, the Son of God, promised to do whatever we ask in His name (John 14:13–14) and the

Father will give whatever we ask in Jesus' name (John 15:16, 16:23). After that, the disciples healed many sicknesses and committed many miraculous signs and wonders in the name of Jesus.

Another important reason that God gives the name Jesus to us is so that we will carry the "name of Jesus" before the Gentiles and their kings and before the people of Israel (Acts 9:15), that Jesus' name might be proclaimed all over the earth (Rom 9:17; Exod 9:16; Deut 32:3; Ps 83:18; Isa 64:2).

Among the many miracles Jesus performed during His ministry in the world, only the familiar miracle of "five loaves of bread and two fish" is written in all four Gospels (Matt 14:15–21; Mark 6:35–44; Luke 9:12–17; John 6:1–13). As you know, words or phrases that are written repeatedly in the Bible are very important. Though pastors can preach many different sermons on the above text, the most important spiritual teaching is, in the words of the Lord Jesus, that "You give them something to eat." What we have to give to those who are spiritually starving to death is the very Word, the bread of life, which is "the very name of Jesus!" Though we do not have gold or silver, we can give what we have, "the name Jesus," to as many people as possible. Sharing Jesus' name is "the very preaching of the Gospel" to the ends of the earth.

The enemy—Satan—threatens people not to speak or teach at all in the name of Jesus because the devil fears and hates the name Jesus (Acts 4:17–18, 5:28). We are not to be deceived by such threats from the devil. It is all right for us to call upon the Lord in our prayers because we are aware that the Lord means the One and Only Trinity of God, and "the name of the Lord" holds the power of salvation. When we pray, however, we can say the "the name of the Lord" because this is "the very Jesus," but it is much better to call out "Jesus!" or "Lord Jesus!" instead of the "Lord!" only.

In my experience, most of the pastors in the United States and Europe, especially in Germany where I live, do not say, "I pray in the name of Jesus" at the end of the prayer. They just say "Amen!" or close a prayer by saying, "I pray in the name of the Lord." Do you know how many "lords" (not *the* Lord) there are in this world? Even King Nebuchadnezzar who confessed and praised our God as the God of gods and the Lord of kings said that he never served only the One and Only God. He was a polytheist (Daniel 2–4). Likewise, it seems that there are a lot of polytheists among churchgoers today.

In conclusion, we are afflicted because of "the Gospel" and "the name of Jesus," but we have to be joyful to participate in the sufferings of Christ and make up our minds to die for the name of Jesus. If we are insulted because of the name of Christ, we are blessed, for the Spirit of glory and of God rests on us (Acts 5:41, 21:13; 2 Tim 1:8; 1 Pet 4:13–14). We have to do everything in "the name of the Lord Jesus," whatever we do, whether in word or in deed (Col 3:17). We have to baptize in "the name of the Lord Jesus" instead of "the name of the Father, of the Son, and of the Holy Spirit." Therefore, we have to kneel down before the Father, and pray and thank Him for giving us "the name of Jesus" (Eph 3:14–15).

To summarize, I believe you understand why our God the Lord considers His name "Jesus" to be so valuable and important. God the Lord commanded us not to misuse the name of the Lord our God (Exod 20:7), and anyone who blasphemes the name of the Lord with a curse must be put to death (Lev 24:11, 16).

As the Word of God is His name (Rev 19:13), when the Israelites did not obey the Word of God, it was the equivalent of blaspheming the Name of God (1 Tim 6:1; Titus 2:5). God rejected even the temple of Solomon where the name of God existed (1 Kgs 9:3–7; 2 Chr 7:16–20), and let the enemy of the Lord burn His sanctuary to the ground and defile the dwelling place of His Name (Ps 74:7–10).

If we do not obey the Word of God, He says, "God's name is blasphemed among the Gentiles because of you" (Rom 2:23–24). Therefore, we must absolutely never blaspheme, defile, profane (Jer 34:16; Ezek 20:39), or show contempt for the name of God (Mal 1:6). Because the beast (the devil) opened his mouth to blaspheme and slander the name of God (Rev 13:6) and he will be cursed (Mal 2:2).

The Name of the Lord our God, Jesus is:

- Glorious and awesome (Deut 28:58; 1 Chr 29:13)
- Great" (Josh 7:9; 1 Sam 12:22; 2 Chr 6:32; Ps 76:1)
- Great and awesome (Ps 99:3)
- Exalted (Ps 148:13)
- Holy (Ps 30:4; 111:9; Isa 29:23; Ezek 20:9, 39)
- Good (Ps 52:9, 54:6)
- Majestic (Ps 81:1, 9)

Therefore, we, as the people and children of God, must:

- Trust in and believe in (Ps 20:7; John 1:12)
- Declare (Ps 22:22)
- Exalt (Ps 34:3; Isa 12:4)
- Sing for joy (Ps 89:12, 16)
- Fear (Deut 28:58; Ps 61:5, 86:11, 102:15)
- Love (Ps 5:11, 69:36; Isa 56:6)
- Give thanks (1 Chr 16:35)
- Glorify (Ps 86:9, 12; 96:8; Isa 63:14; 2 Thess 1:12; Rev 15:4)
- Praise (Ps 30:4, 44:8, 72:19)

His glorious Name forever!

"The Name" of God itself is not a person but it is no problem even if "the Name" is treated as a person because "the Name Jesus" shows the *personality of God* and *represents the person, God.* For example, the Bible describes the Name of the Lord as a person, as in, "See, the Name of the Lord comes from afar" (Isa 30:27).

Why do you think the Lord commanded us to praise "the Name" instead of "the Lord, your God" or simply "the Lord" and "God"? Isn't it wonderful that the Trinity of God who came into our hearts with the Name of Jesus to be with us forever wants to be praised by all He created? He longs to be in heaven together with us who are His brides by baptizing with one Spirit into one body.

19

The Holy Spirit and Christ

THE WORDS, "God our Savior," are written three times in Titus (1:3, 2:10, 3:4), and can be found in 1 Timothy 1:1 as well. They can also be found as "God my Savior" in the so-called "Magnificat" of Luke 1:47. Similar terminology is found in the following Titus references:

- Christ Jesus our Savior (1:4)
- Jesus Christ our Savior (3:6)
- Our great God and Savior, Jesus Christ (2:13)

The above language means that Jesus Christ (or Christ Jesus), the Son of God, is our Savior. The meaning of "God" in "God our Savior" as mentioned first (Titus 1:3, 2:10, 3:4) might mean "Jesus Christ, the Son of God who is also God Himself and Savior" according to Titus 2:13.

However, the meaning of "God" from "God my Savior" in Luke 1:47 is "the One and Only God" because "Jesus, the Son of God" has not yet been born. In addition, the "the Trinity of God—Father, the Son and the Holy Spirit" has not yet been revealed.

It is important to note that the words "our" or "my" preceding "Savior God or Lord" are written more frequently in the Old Testament than in the New Testament. The Israelites called "God," "God our Savior" (1 Chr 16:35;

Ps 25:5, 79:9; Isa 60:16) even before "Jesus Christ, the Son of God" was born.

We know the meaning of "Christ Jesus" or "Jesus Christ." "Jesus" is "the name" and "Christ" indicates that He has a "duty or job" to complete. "Christ" is the Greek translation of the Hebrew "Messiah" which means "the Anointed One." Anointing is done to a king, prophet, priest, or Messiah for the purpose of fulfilling a specific mission. Thus, "Christ" is translated as "the Savior" and "Jesus Christ," which means "Jesus is Savior."

Do you think "the Son of God" who came to this world in the flesh two thousand years ago was only "Jesus Christ?" In our own consciousness, we are apt to think only the Son of God is Jesus Christ. In another words, "the Son of God" is "only the Savior." From the viewpoint of the history of salvation, we, of course, have to honor and love the Son of God who shed blood on the cross for the redemption of our sins. But, as mentioned repeatedly, the Son of God alone cannot achieve salvation. It is the mutual work of the Trinity of God. The Father has chosen, the Son redeemed by shedding blood, and the Holy Spirit sealed as a deposit of guarantee, and this completes the work of salvation (Eph 1:4, 7, 13). From this viewpoint, the Trinity of God (the Father, the Son, and the Holy Spirit) collectively is "Savior," which means "the Christ." And, as the name of the Trinity of God is "Jesus," the Trinity of God is all "Jesus Christ." This clarifies the mystery of the one body of the Trinity of God. Therefore, "Jesus Christ is the same yesterday and today and forever" (Heb 13:8).

The following is an excerpt from Peter's sermon in Acts 3:19–20:

> Repent, then, and turn to God, so that your sins may be wiped out, that times of refreshing may come from the Lord, and that he may

send the Christ, who has been appointed for you—even Jesus.

In short, if you repent and turn to God, the Lord will send "Christ Jesus" to you. It is understood that this "Christ Jesus" is neither "the Son of God with flesh," because "the Son of God with flesh" has already gone to heaven, nor "the second coming of Jesus," because during "the second coming of Jesus," He will appear as "the Lord of Judgment," not as "the God of salvation." Even though it is beyond our understanding, the above is written in parallel context to Acts 2:38, "Repent and be baptized, and you will receive the Holy Spirit."

Therefore, based on the above verse, the meaning of "Christ Jesus" is "the Counselor, the Holy Spirit with the Name of Jesus who is also the Spirit of Jesus Christ carrying out the works of Jesus Christ."

The Apostle Paul said in 1 Corinthians 5:4:

> When you are assembled in the name of our Lord Jesus and I am with you in spirit, and the power of our Lord Jesus is present.

In this phrase, "the power of our Lord Jesus" is actually "the power of the Holy Spirit" who is also "the Spirit of Jesus."

In 2 Corinthians 13:5, it reads:

> Do you not realize that Christ Jesus is in you—unless, of course, you fail the test?

In this phrase, "Christ Jesus" is actually "the Spirit of Jesus Christ," which means that it is impossible to enter the kingdom of heaven unless "the Counselor, the Holy Spirit with Jesus' name" is in you.

Theologian James Packer, made two related comments in his book *Keep in Step with the Spirit*:

> Nothing is new here save that I am highlighting the Christ centeredness of all these deeds of the Spirit in a way that is not always done.[1]
>
> As knowing the Holy Spirit means precisely knowing Christ, so honoring the Holy Spirit means precisely honoring Christ.[2]

Now, I would like to propose the following in order to avoid an unnecessary dispute. That is, we understand that "the Son of God" who came into this world in the flesh as "Jesus Christ" is the narrow meaning and "the Trinity of God" as "Jesus Christ" as the broader meaning."

I give praise and glorify to the Trinity of God, our Savior forever!

---

1. Packer, *Keep In Step With the Spirit*, 56.
2. Ibid., 260.

20

The Holy Spirit and the Word

EVERY RELIGION in the world today has its own canon—a set of religious writings regarded as authentic and definitive and forming a religion's body of scripture. There is no religion without a canon. As Christianity is based on the life of Jesus rather than on doctrine, Christianity, appropriately, is placed in the category of religion. I would like to compare the canons of other religions to prove that the Bible—the canon of Christianity—contains more authority than the canons of other religions, even when taking an objective view.

Normally, the canons of other religions are written by a few people and in a short time. On the other hand, approximately forty people spanning a period of more than 1,600 years wrote the Bible. The reason the Bible, which is thought to be written by many people in different times and places, is concentrated on one theme, namely Jesus, is that the Bible is inspired by one author, the Holy Spirit, who transcends space and time.(Isa 34:16; 2 Tim 3:16; 2 Peter 1:21; Psalm 19:1–4). The Bible is the only single-volume book to have sold more than one billion copies, and continues to maintain its status as *the* all-time bestseller.[1] Unlike the founders of

---

1. Winston, "Bibles and Sacred Texts," line 17.

other religions, only the Son of God, Jesus, was born after this event was prophesied in the Bible. Christians not only acknowledge the authority of the Bible for such objective reasons, but because we believe that the Bible is the very Word of God.

Many are familiar with passages that talk about Jesus, the Son of God:

- In the beginning was the Word, and the Word was with God, and the Word was God. (John 1:1)
- The Word became flesh and made his dwelling among us. (John 1:14)
- In the past God spoke to our forefathers through the prophets at many times and in various ways, but in these last days he has spoken to us by his Son, whom he appointed heir of all things and through whom he made the universe. (Heb 1:1–2)

In one short chapter it is impossible to explain or discuss every aspect of "the Word" and "God," so I will focus on some key elements that help bring understanding to the "the Word of God."

First, it is crucial to comprehend the concept of what it means to say, "I believe in God" or "I believe in Jesus." Many churchgoers, even longtime attendees, do not know what it means to "believe in God." How can someone say, "I believe in God" whom they have never seen or touched, and "I believe in Jesus" whom they have never met? The answer is simple: believe in "the written Word of God" and obey "the Word of God." If we say, "I believe God," that means we believe "the power of God." But if we say, "I believe in God," it means we believe "the Word of God" or "the Word spoken by God." In other words, we believe in His personality.

Second, the purpose of the Word of God is to gain souls for *salvation* (2 Tim 3:15) and *life* (John 20:31). Jesus, the Son of God, said, "The words I have spoken to you are spirit and they are life" (John 6:63). He also said that He is "the bread of life" (John 6:35, 48). and "life" itself (John 14:6). Jesus, the Son of God, gives people life through the written word of God, namely "His own words."

Third, the Word of God is considered the word of blessing; the Gospel means good news and blessed news. The Bible speaks so abundantly of the blessings of heaven and earth that they are unable to be counted. For example:

> You may enjoy good health and all may go with you, even as your soul is getting along well. (3 John 1:2)

However, please keep in mind that blessings are poured out to us when we obey the Word of God, and conversely, the curse will come upon you unless you obey the Word of God. The Lord said, in Deuteronomy 30:19: "I have set before you life and death, blessings and curses" and it is up to us to choose one of them.

Fourth, the Word of God will certainly be accomplished (Num 23:19; Isa 40:8, 55:11; Matt 5:18, 24:35). God created the heavens and the earth with the word (Gen 1:1; Heb 11:3), and will let them be judged by fire with the same word (2 Pet 3:7). Those of the Christian faith believe that the prophetic Word of God has nearly been achieved and that the second coming of Jesus will surely be accomplished soon.

In addition to the above, I would like to emphasize that the word we are talking about holds the same power of creation and destruction as the Word of God. After God created man in his own image, He let man subdue the earth and rule over all the living creatures on the ground (Gen 1:28). The instrument used to rule over living creatures was "the word." For example, we bring up our children on the word, teach school with the word, run companies with the word, command armies with the word, and rule over countries with the word. And, of course, the church builds up the Kingdom of God with words—those that we use, as well as the Word of God. Therefore, Psalm 119, the longest chapter in the Bible, is full of the Words of God regarding laws, decrees, commands, precepts, etc.

In the beginning, the word had the power of creation. After the fall of man, it also had the power of destruction. Since then, the devil continues to deprave mankind with the word, especially using slanderous intrigue. The Lord teaches that, "The tongue has the power of life and death, and those who love it will eat its fruit" (Prov 18:21), and a man lives with "the fruit of his lips" (Prov 12:14, 13:2), or "the fruit of his mouth" (Prov 18:20). These verses in Proverbs especially illustrate that the word contains lots of power. The word has the power to restore health, family, church, business, and even the country. "The tongue that brings healing is a tree of life, but a deceitful tongue crushes the spirit" (Prov 15:4).

It is important to know why the Lord commanded us to eagerly desire the gift of prophecy over many other spiritual gifts (1 Cor 14:1, 5, 39). As taught, He knew that prophecy that is proclaimed with faith in the name of Jesus would definitely be accomplished:

> Now faith is being sure of what we hope for and certain of what we do not see. (Hebrews 11:1)

In addition, he who prophesies edifies the church. Therefore, we are encouraged to speak creative, blessed, edifying, kind, and admirable words. May only words of praise, glorification, and thanksgiving to the Lord our God come from our mouth.

Now, I would like to demonstrate that the writer of the Word of God is the Holy Spirit, and explain how the Holy Spirit works through the words.

The Bible testifies that the author of the Word of God is the Holy Spirit (Isa 34:16; 2 Tim 3:16–17; 2 Pet 1:20–21). It is written that, "the Holy Spirit spoke long ago through the mouth of David" (Acts 1:16 and "the Holy Spirit spoke the truth to your forefathers when he said through Isaiah the prophet" (Acts 28:25), In addition, the Bible said that "the Word of God" is the same as "the Holy Spirit." In Acts 10:47, it is written as "They have received the Holy Spirit" and the identical event is written as, "They had received the Word of God" in next chapter, Acts 11:1. I have already explained in chapter 4, *The Holy Spirit and the Trinity* that "the Word" is one of the most vital facts because it confirms the Trinity of God as one.

The Bible also tells us "the Word of God" is "the sword of the Spirit" (Eph 6:17). No matter how good the sword, it is of no use unless we use it. No matter how much life and power the Word of God gives, it is of no use unless we obey the Word of God. When the Spirit is working through the written Word of God, the Word of God can be living and active. It can be sharper than any double-edged sword that penetrates, even to the point of dividing the soul and spirit, joints and marrow; and it can judge the thoughts and attitudes of the heart (Heb 4:12).

The following words illustrate that the Holy Spirit uses the Word of God as His sword: "and out of his mouth came a sharp double-edged sword" (Rev 1:16), "the sword of my mouth" (Rev 2:16), "Out of his mouth comes a sharp sword" (Rev 19:15), and "the sword that came out of the mouth of the rider on the horse" (Rev 19:21). These words illustrate that the Holy Spirit uses the Word of God as His sword.

We can also see that the Holy Spirit—the author of the Word of God, the Word itself, and who works through the Word—speaks through the angels sometimes but primarily speaks personally through the prophets and servants of the

Lord. The word "Lord" (*YHWH*) is written as "the Spirit" in some places in the Bible:

The Lord	The Spirit
Psalm 78:40	Isaiah 63:10
Psalm 95:7–11	Hebrews 3:7–11
Isaiah 6:9–10	Acts 28:25–26
Jeremiah 31:33–34	Hebrews 10:15–17

The Word of God was written through the prophets who were moved by the Holy Spirit, but most of the Old Testament was transcribed as the Lord spoke personally. Old Testament Scriptures often begin or end with phrases such as, "the Lord said to Abraham," "the Lord said to Moses," "says the Lord," and "declares the Lord Almighty."

In these clauses, we can understand "the Lord" as "the Trinity of God," or it might be reasonable to conclude that "the Lord" is "God the Father" because the Old Testament was the era of God the Father. However, Ezekiel 11:5 states:

> Then the Spirit of the Lord came upon me, and he told me to say.

Here, the Holy Spirit came directly upon Ezekiel and spoke to him personally. This is also the case in Ezekiel 3:22, 24. As I said before, because the Lord is "the Spirit," it is probable that all the words were actually spoken by the Holy Spirit.

I would like to give a supplementary lesson about the book of "Haggai." It is clear that the Word of the Lord came to the prophet Haggai because there are lots of references to "the Lord Almighty" in each of only two chapters in this short book. Haggai 1:14 reports: "So the Lord stirred up the spirits of the remnant of the people," while the words "stirred up" are written as "moved" in 2 Chronicles 36:22. Both originate from the Hebrew "*ur.*" We know that the Holy Spirit within the Trinity of God can "stir up" or "move" hearts and spirits, therefore, the Lord means the Holy Spirit!

"'I am with you,' declares the Lord" (Hag 1:13), "'For I am with you,' declares the Lord Almighty" (Hag 2:4), and "my Spirit remains among you. Do not fear" (Hag 2:5) can also be found. The words "I am with you" relate to "And surely I am with you always, to the very end of the age," which is the last promise our Lord Jesus made before He was taken up to heaven (Matt 28:20). Jesus promised to come again as "the Spirit of Jesus" and dwell with us forever (John 16:16–22). The one who dwells within us forever is "the Holy Spirit" and He exists as the "eternal present." To reiterate, the Lord means the Holy Spirit!

In the Old Testament, there are many references to "the word," including "the Word of the Lord came to me" (Ezek 3:16, 7:1) and "The Word of the Lord came to me, saying . . . " (Jer 1:4). In these instances, "The Word of the Lord" is personified. "The Word of the Lord" itself is not a person, but because the Bible indicates "the Word" as "God" (John 1:1), many of the words described are as a "person." Here are some examples:

- The Lord continued to appear at Shiloh, and there he revealed himself to Samuel through his word. (1 Sam 3:21)
- Because you have rejected the word of the Lord, he has rejected you as king. (1 Sam 15:23, 26)
- In God, whose word I praise (Ps 56:4)
- In the Lord, whose word I praise (Ps 56:10)
- Till the word of the Lord proved him true (Ps 105:19)
- For they have rebelled against the words of God (Ps 107:11)

- He sent forth his word and healed them (Ps 107:20)
- He sends his word and melts them (Ps 147:18)
- The Gentiles also had received the word of God (Acts 11:1)
- Now I commit you to God and to the word of his grace (Acts 20:32)
- Sustaining all things by his powerful word (Heb 1:3)

In the minor prophets, the Lord is indicated as a "vision" (Obad 1:1; Mic 1:1; Nah 1:1; Hab 2:3) or "oracle" (Nah 1:1; Hab 1:1; Mal 1:1) instead of the Word of God, and both "vision" and "oracle" signify "the Word of God" (Mic 1:1; Mal 1:1). The word "vision" is translated as "revelation" in Proverbs 29:18.

The question, then, is how can the Word of God or the vision or the oracle come upon servants of the Lord? As previously discussed, the word "Lord" actually means the Holy Spirit—all designate the words of the Holy Spirit. Both "vision" and "revelation" belong to the works of the Holy Spirit as a part of the Trinity of God (Joel 2:28; Eph 1:17). Keep in mind that the Holy Spirit Himself is the Word and that He has spoken many times personally, not only in the Old Testament but also in the New Testament.

In the Old Testament, God, appearing as an image, often came down to the earth and talked with the servants of the Lord (Gen 18; Num 12:8). At that time, "God as an image" did not come in the flesh as Jesus the Son of God did in the New Testament. This appearance of God was a kind of manifestation. Simply put, God came to the earth as an image with the help of the Holy Spirit just like Jesus came to the earth with the power of the Holy Spirit.

In Revelation chapters 2 and 3, there is a scene where Jesus, the Son of God, talks to the angels of the seven churches in Asia. The scene finishes with, "He who has an ear, let him hear what the Spirit says to the churches." In reality this is what the Holy Spirit said to the churches. The word of Jesus, the Son of God, is the very word of the Holy Spirit because the Holy Spirit is the Spirit of Jesus!

Therefore, from now on, we must live on every word that comes from the mouth of God (Matt 4:4), meditate on the law of the Lord not only day and night (Ps 1:2), but also all day long (Ps 119:97). We need help from the Holy Spirit, the writer of the Word, so that we fully understand it. We are encouraged to pray to the Holy Spirit on all occasions and with all kinds of prayers and requests (Eph 6:18; Jude 20). The Holy Spirit is filled with joy and happiness when we read the Bible, the Word of God. If comparing a cart to a healthy church life, the two wheels of the cart would be "word" and "prayer." Actually the Word and prayer should always be lived together. If we are inclined to the Word alone, it is easy for us to fall into legalism. On the other hand, if we are inclined only toward prayer, we can easily fall into mysticism.

Let us be grateful to the Lord who gives us the Bible, the book of the books. Praise to the Trinity of God who is the Word! Praise to the Son of God, Jesus who is the Word that became flesh! Praise to the Holy Spirit who wrote the Word, is himself the Word and uses the Word as a sword!

21

Holy Spirit, My Love!

God is love. (1 John 4:8, 16)

THE ABOVE words express very well who God is. Therefore, people often say that Christianity is "the religion of love." We are told to love above all things. I have preached the Gospel of love most frequently and heard about it the most, too. But love is not a word exclusive to Christianity.

Love seems to be the most popular motif of literary works or works of art even by "worldly people." A Korean pastor in America said, during a revival, that he had studied hundreds of Korean lyrics and found the word "love" in all of them. Love is a common theme in movies and drama as well. The world is filled with love even without God.

There are lots of impressive love stories in arts and literature. Sometimes the love appears much more beautiful than Christian love; people even risk their lives for love. Sometimes I am moved to tears watching a movie or drama. I remember one supporting actress in a Korean TV drama who weeps very often because the boy she loves so deeply is pursuing another girl. At one time, with tears in her eyes, she told the boy, "I will wait until you come back to me. Please understand that my heart is with you always. I will come running to you any time you want."

At that moment I realized, "Ah! She has a heart after God!" I realized that even one who does not believe in God can have a heart for God. It is the same heart of a father who eagerly awaits the return of his son who has left the house (Luke 15:11–32). Having a heart of God is possible even without knowing God because God created all people according to His image and likeness (Gen 1:26–27).

Almost every problem that happens in the world is actually due to love. Causes range from being unable to love, to not being loved, to refusing to accept the love of God. In addition to falling on worldly people who do not know the love of God, the issue afflicts Christians who have tasted the love of God.

Serious problems that plague the world in which we live include jealousy, envy, hate, quarrels, war, murder, robbery, adultery, rape, violence, gambling, drugs, and more. Do you know that most of these sins are owing to a lack of God's love? Even those who appear to love little, love in their own way. No matter how much a man hates his brothers, he often deeply loves his children. No matter how much he hates neighboring countries, he loves his native land. This is called having love your own way and it is a distorted kind of love. The devil is a master at distorting pure love, which is the love of God.

Even then, it is necessary to ask ourselves whether we truly know the love of God, even though we are people of God. How is the love of God defined? Do we really love one another with the love of God?

I saw an American movie a long time ago where the lead actor, who was a millionaire, bought a huge mansion with lots of rooms, a big garden, a swimming pool, and other expensive amenities. Yet when he was standing alone on the terrace, he looked so lonely. Why? There was no love shared in his house. Seeing the scene, I thought of the kingdom of heaven.

I believe the kingdom of heaven, the house of the Lord, our God, is so magnificent, beautiful, and splendid that it is unimaginably incomparable to that mansion. Even the cosmos and the earth that God created Himself and saw that it was good are nothing compared with the kingdom of heaven. Suppose that there is no one in the beautiful kingdom of heaven right now except God alone! How lonesome and desolate is He? Please imagine that you are in the kingdom of heaven alone! You surely believe that a small cottage with someone you love is much better than the kingdom of heaven without anyone to love.

God cannot help but love. Life is unbearable without loving someone; He has to love someone and has to be loved by someone. For this reason He has chosen us with His life in order to love us, as well as to be loved by us (Matt 22:37–38; Luke 10:27; John 3:16; Rom 5:5–8).

There is a problem with the flow of love. Love is at its best when both parties are able to love at the same level. For example, a man does not love an ant. There are fewer problems if the level of love between a man and woman is similar, to say nothing of the fact that it is impossible to love God in the same way He loves us because God is the Creator and He created man. But God jumped over the wall. The very nature of God became a human being through His Son, Jesus! But there is another wall and it is *sin*! God, in His righteousness, cannot dwell with sinners. Therefore, He washed away all our sins with the blood of Jesus in order that we may love one another.

God granted a great concession and poured out His wonderful love in order to make us His lover. Do we really know the love of God—the kind of love that makes it possible for us to love at His level?

The love of God, the Father, is the love that has given His One and Only Son to us unsparingly. In a life and death situation, is there anyone among us who would send one of his sons to die rather than be willing to die himself? If he had a choice, a father would rather die than let his son suffer that fate. But God, the Father, gave up His One and Only Son! God made a tremendous sacrifice for sinners—the entire human race—though each is not much better than a worm. He gave up His son for what some might consider *a great waste*! Has God, the Father, *wasted* His love? Have you ever *wasted* anything for your lover? Have you ever loved someone so much that you would give up your life, or all that you own, for them? Would you waste something as precious as a priceless jar of perfume for love, as the woman in Bethany did when she poured expensive perfume over Jesus (Matt 26:6–13)? She understood that he had to die and was willing to give up her priceless perfume to prepare Him for burial.

God, the Son, gave His one and only life for us—His love was, and continues to be, "life-giving." The Son, who is the Lord, personally put love into practice as He said:

> Greater love has no one than this that he lay down his life for his friends. (John 15:13)

Have you ever risked your life for love? You might be willing to give up your life for someone you really love, such as your parents, children, or dear friends. But would you risk your life for someone you consider to be worthless? As a people, are we powerless sinners, and God's enemies, as stated in the Bible (Rom 5:6, 8, 10)? Are we less valuable than even the worthless? For as long as we live, shouldn't we love the Lord who loved us enough to become life giving?

God, the Spirit, came into our hearts and is living within us, even though we are sinners. Please remember that we are, by nature, objects of wrath (Eph 2:3). The Holy Spirit is holy as He stands. He is "the Spirit of Holiness!" The Spirit of God wants to live with us forever in spite of the fact that we are sinners who are filled with wicked, deceitful, and evil thoughts (Gen 6:5; Ps 51:5; Jer 17:9; Matt 15:19; Rom 3:10–23, 7:14–24)!

In truth, the Holy Spirit's action of coming into our hearts is abnormal because man has treated the Lord so cruelly. The Old Testament book of Hosea lends insight into the situation. What man in this world would take his wife back, a woman like Gomer who played the harlot even after she bore him three children? Are we any better or holier than Gomer? We must never despise the love of the Holy Spirit who comes into our heart and dwells forever.

The Holy Spirit cannot stand it if we love other people or other things more than Him. We must remember that the Holy God is the Lord; He is a jealous God (Exod 34:14). Even the waters and rivers cannot quench the flame of jealousy (Song 8:7). Please imagine that your beloved wife loves another man or that your beloved husband loves another woman. How can you sleep with such terrible jealousy or evil thoughts about harming the other person? How much stronger, then, is the jealousy of the Holy Spirit who is truly holy, as compared to the jealousy of us unholy sinners? The Holy Spirit wants to be loved one hundred percent by us, nothing less, not even ninety-nine percent!

By the way, whom do you want to be loved by?

I used to love a girl one-sidedly when I was young. There was not much of a romantic atmosphere for young boys and girls to meet easily in Korea at that time. It was painful to love one-sidedly and, to make matters worse, that girl loved another man. I suffered more pain and misery than anyone who has never experienced such a thing could imagine. In Korea, it is said that he who has never loved one-sidedly is not qualified to discuss life. The words I wanted most to hear from that girl were, "Mr. Kim, I love you, too!"

Whom do you really want to be loved by?

It is important to understand why our Lord asks us to "Love the Lord your God with all your heart and with all your soul and with all your mind" (Matt 22:37). Everyone likes to love and be loved in return. We love our children and long to be loved by them. We do not care to be loved by those we do not love and, whenever possible, avoid being in their company.

The Lord our God would really like to be loved by us in the same way because He loves us with all His heart and with all His soul and with all His mind (John 3:16). Who is He? Isn't He the eternal, almighty, omnipresent King of kings, and Lord of lords who created the heavens and the earth with the Word? Who are we? Aren't we naturally the worst of the sinners who are headed straight to hell? Notwithstanding, God, the King of kings dares us to love Him! He makes each one of us His bride! And He says to me, "Arise, my darling, my beautiful one, and come with me" (Song 2:10, 13).

Normally, there are no secrets between lovers. Both parties share personally about themselves and want to give everything they have to each other. God has given us all the blessings He has, even His one and only Son! He has given His Kingdom to us as an inheritance. He has prepared all the crowns and rewards in heaven for His bride. However, the Holy Spirit loves us so much that He is heartbroken because He cannot show Himself to us—He is invisible. Therefore, He shows His love to us through the use of descriptive titles such as Father, Son, friend, Jesus Christ, truth, God, helper, Counselor, Lord, etc. He also demonstrates His love through manifestations such as different spiritual gifts. These are just a few of the ways he says, "Don't you know how much I love you?"

I want you to feel the love of the Holy Spirit with your heart seeing His various works.

James 4:5 offers understanding of the emotions experience by the Holy Spirit as it reads:

> Or do you think Scripture says without reason
> that the Spirit he caused to live in us envies
> intensely?

The above means that the Holy Spirit living in us loves us very much, but on the other hand, He envies intensely, too. He cannot stand it if we love other things or other people more than Him because He has emotions and loathes being ignored or neglected or despised!

The following Scripture, Song of Songs 8:6b, helps to explain how the Holy Spirit feels:

> for love is as strong as death,
>   its jealousy unyielding as the grave.
>   It burns like blazing fire,
>   like a mighty flame.

The above passage holds the same meaning as the previous James verse but is more powerful and expresses a stronger tone. God loves us so much but His jealousy is also as strong and mighty as death or a blazing fire. In Nahum 1:2 it is written: "The Lord is a jealous and avenging God." Love, according to the Bible, is not true love without jealousy. The love of the Holy Spirit is the love of jealousy like a blazing fire.

"God is love" also means "the Father, the Son and the Holy Spirit is love." Romans 5:5 reads:

> And hope does not disappoint us, because God
> has poured out his love into our hearts by the
> Holy Spirit, whom he has given us.

We now know that the Holy Spirit prompts the love of God. That is why it is written as "the love of the Spirit" (Romans 15:30) and love is the first fruit of the Holy Spirit (Gal 5:22). Therefore, we can also say "the Holy Spirit is love" as well as "God is love."

Each and every day, I encourage you to confess your love to the Holy Spirit, who is true God and true Lord with the Name of Jesus, a person Himself, and one who is completing every salvation work.

Holy Spirit, I love you!

Epilogue

In the era of Jesus, the Son of God, the priests, scribes, and Pharisees thought they believed in God and were serving Him well, yet they killed Jesus by placing Him in the hands of the Gentiles. They mistakenly thought they were offering a service to God, because they did not know the Father or the Son (John 16:2–3). Unfortunately, the Trinity of God had not been clearly revealed to them at that time. They knew nothing of the relationship between the Father and the Son and, therefore, killed the Son of God. Sadly, the same thing is happening at the present time, even though Scripture clearly spells out the Trinity of God.

The fact is that people and churches that profess to believe devoutly in God or Jesus continue to persecute and despise believers who participate in today's "Spirit-oriented movement." The same thing happened in Jesus' day:

> At that time the son born in the ordinary way persecuted the son born by the power of the Spirit. It is the same now. (Gal 4:29)

Persecution occurred because they did not understand the relationship between the Son and the Holy Spirit.

As mentioned in the first chapter, many churches are still ill informed about the Holy Spirit and, therefore, ignore, neglect, despise, and even profane Him. Servants of the Lord, especially pastors and theologians, should not overlook this fact. It is time to face reality, to get to know the Holy Spirit better, and to honor Him more. The salvation of souls is too important to yield a single point, and the role of the Holy Spirit in salvation is too critical to ignore. Without guidance from the Holy Spirit, no one can recognize sin (John 16:7–9), no one can come to Jesus (John 16:13), and no one can testify to Jesus (John 15:26), which means that no one can come to the Father in heaven (John 14:6) and no one can be saved.

Now, the churches have to hear the voice of the Holy Spirit (Rev 2; 3) and servants of the Lord must also be sensitive to His voice. The voice of the Holy Spirit is nothing but the voice of Jesus and the voice of God the Father, which is the written Word of God. We have already learned that one of the important facts that makes up the Trinity of God is "the Word." Therefore, if we despise "the Word of God," we despise the Holy Spirit Himself; Jesus, the Son of God Himself; and God, the Father Himself. Surely we must love "the Word" in order to love "the Holy Spirit!"

There are so many books available on pneumatology that choosing the right one can be confusing. Despising the Holy Spirit is a major concern, but so is being confused about the Holy Spirit. The devil loves to deceive. He knows that his time is short (Rev 12:12) and he is trying to hinder the works of the Holy Spirit in order to postpone the completion of salvation—the second coming of the Lord. We must not be cheated by the devil's deception.

Campbell Morgan said this in his book *The Spirit of God*:

> To borrow Dr. Steele's phrase, the Conservator of orthodoxy in every successive age is the Holy Spirit. Creeds do not ensure orthodoxy, for no individual church holds all the truth of the Church.[1]

---

1. Morgan, *The Spirit of God*, 148–49.

Church leaders, especially, must listen carefully to the above statement because too many denominations and seminaries are overflowing with students who are being taught wrong pneumatology. It is urgent that the correct pneumatolgy be taught throughout the world.

As our Lord Jesus said, because of an increase in wickedness, the love of most will grow cold as the end draws near (Matt 24:12). Our enemy, the devil, prowls around like a roaring lion looking for someone to devour (1 Pet 5:8), not the world, but the churches (saints). We might be deceived unless we practice self-control and are alert. Christians who have the name of Jesus will never enjoy a successful church life without the fullness of the Holy Spirit and there is no fullness of the Holy Spirit without help from the Holy Spirit.

The first and greatest commandment of Jesus is to love the Lord our God with all our heart and with all our soul and with all our mind, and the second is to love our neighbor as ourselves (Matt 22:37–39). It is absolutely impossible for us to love without the help of the Holy Spirit because love is the first fruit of the Holy Spirit (Gal 5:22) and the Holy Spirit is the Spirit of love. (Rom 15:30; Col 1:8) Among faith, hope, and love, the greatest is love (1 Cor 13:13) and love is the fulfillment of the law (Rom 13:10). How can we love without help from the Holy Spirit and how can we fulfill the law without help from the Holy Spirit? How can we have a successful church life without the manifestations of the Holy Spirit and fruit of the Holy Spirit? It is imperative that we acknowledge, welcome, honor, exalt, and love the Holy Spirit because He is a person and has great emotion.

If we are really servants of the Lord, we are called to attend to the Holy Spirit in the following ways:

- Listen to His voice and do not grieve Him (Eph 4:30)
- Not put out the Spirit's fire (1 Thess 5:19)
- Live by the Spirit (Gal 5:16)
- Be led by the Spirit (Gal 5:18)
- Have the fruit of the Spirit (Gal 5:22–23)
- Keep in step with the Spirit (Gal 5:25)

We can then be filled with the Holy Spirit (Eph 5:18) and become witnesses to the ends of the earth with the power of the Holy Spirit. (Acts 1:8)

It is my sincere hope that Korean churches serve as a role model among the churches in the world, teaching the right knowledge and right works of the Holy Spirit through this small, thought insufficient, book. There are many gods (Deut 4:28; Jer 11:13; Acts 19:26) and lords in this world but there is only one "God of gods," "Lord of lords," "King of kings" (Deut 10:17; Ps 136:2–3; Dan 2:47; 1 Tim 6:15; Rev 17:14, 19:16) and only one true God. (Jer 10:10) The Lord means "the invisible God" (Col 1:15) who is the very "I AM WHO I AM" (Exod 3:14) and there is only one "Holy Spirit" whose name is "Jesus" in this world! The Bible says, "Blessed is the nation whose God is the Lord." (Ps 33:12, 144:15)

Therefore, we must acknowledge the Lord who is the Holy Spirit (Hos 6:3) so that we are not destroyed from lack of knowledge (Hos 4:6). Then, the earth will be "*full* of the knowledge of the Lord (Holy Spirit) as the waters cover the sea, (Isa 11:9) as well as "*filled* with the knowledge of the glory of the Lord (Holy Spirit) as the waters cover the sea." (Hab 2:14)

Through this book, I would like all servants of the Lord to take this opportunity to acknowledge, welcome, love, and please the Trinity of God, especially the Holy Spirit. Thus, the Holy Spirit can use His servants to His heart's content in order to fill "the full number of the Gentiles" as well as "the number of fellow servants and brothers who were to be killed." Doing so will shorten the time of the second coming of the Lord Jesus. I really hope the path of our bridegroom Jesus Christ will be straight and as early as possible!

May the grace of the Lord Jesus Christ, and the love of God, and the fellowship of the Holy Spirit be with all the readers of this book!

Bibliography

Berkhof, Hendrikus. *The Doctrine of the Holy Spirit*, Richmond, VA: John Knox Press, 1967.

Fee, Gordon D. *Paul, The Spirit and the People of God*, Peabody, MA: Hendrickson Publishers, 2005.

Ferguson, Sinclair. *The Holy Spirit*, Downers Grove, ILL: InterVarsity Press, 1996.

Graham, Billy. *The Holy Spirit*, Waco, TX: Word Books Publisher, 1979.

Han, Yung-je. *The Dictionary of Christianity*, Seoul, Korea: The Christian Literature Press, 1991.

Hong, Inkyu. "*Paul and the Holy Spirit.*" Reformed Bible Study Summer Semester Lecture, Pastoral Graduate School of the Presbyterian General Assembly, 2002.

Kuyper, Abraham. *The Work of the Holy Spirit*, Grand Rapids, MI: WM. B. Eerdmans Publishing Co., 1975.

Morgan, G. Campbell. *The Spirit of God*, Eugene, OR: Wipf and Stock Publishers, 2003.

Owen, John. *The Holy Spirit*, Ross-Shire, Scotland: Christian Heritage, 2004.

Packer, James I. *Keep in Step With the Spirit*, Old Tappen, NJ: Flemming H. Revell Co., 1984.

Pink, Arthur W. *The Holy Spirit*, Grand Rapids, MI: Baker Books, 1996.

Steele, David N., Thomas, Curtis C. *The Five Points of Calvinism*, Seoul, Korea: Word of Life Press, 1982.

Winston, Kimberly. Publishers Weekly: "Bibles and Sacred Texts." No pages. Accessed May 7, 2007. Online: http://www.publishersweekly.com/article/CA167433.html?q=bible+bestseller+sales.

www.ingramcontent.com/pod-product-compliance
Lightning Source LLC
Chambersburg PA
CBHW072140160426
43197CB00012B/2191